Samba

Arts and Politics of the Everyday
Patricia Mellencamp, Meaghan Morris, Andrew Ross,
series editors

SAMBA

resistance in motion

barbara browning

indiana university press

bloomington and indianapolis

The author gratefully acknowledges the Princeton University
Committee on Research in the Humanities and Social
Sciences for aid in preparing this manuscript.

This book is a publication of

Indiana University Press
601 North Morton Street
Bloomington, IN 47404-3797 USA

http://iupress.indiana.edu

Telephone orders 800-842-6796
Fax orders 812-855-7931
Orders by e-mail iuporder@indiana.edu

The paper used in this publication meets the minimum
requirements of American National Standard for
Information Sciences—Permanence of Paper for Printed
Library Materials, ANSI Z39.48-1984.

∞™

Manufactured in the United States of America

Library of Congress Cataloging-in-Publication Data
Browning, Barbara, date
    Samba : resistance in motion / Barbara Browning.
        p. cm. — (Arts and politics of the everyday)
    Includes bibliographical references and index.
    ISBN 0-253-32867-5 (alk. paper). —
ISBN 0-253-20956-0 (pbk. : alk. paper)
    1. Dance—Social aspects—Brazil. 2. Dance, Black—
Brazil. I. Title. II. Series.
GV1637.B76   1995
306.4'84—dc20   94-38586

    5 6 7 05

For Mãe Aildes, Boa Gente,
and of course Loremil

C O N T E N T S

Introduction

In his beautiful and melancholy, partly autobio-
graphical book on Brazil, *Tristes tropiques,* Claude
Lévi-Strauss reflects on the self-wounding of the anthropologist: "Never will he feel himself to be 'at home'
anywhere. He will always be, psychologically speaking,
an amputated man."[1] Eight years ago, in a particularly
unlikely, moldy closet in an apartment in Brazil, I found
a book that made a similar suggestion in a more allegori-
cal way. It was an old English-language Ace paperback,
a flip-over, double-sided science fiction fantasy. The side
I remember was called *Exile from Xanadu,* and it recounted the adventures of an interplanetary traveler
who was involved in an unfortunate smashup galaxies
from home. He was patched up by the spacelings who
found him, and when he arrived back home the earth
doctor told him, "The aliens did an astounding job on

your reconstruction, considering their limited knowledge of human physiology. Somehow they managed to hook up connections between their prosthetic material and the nerve endings of your . . . uh. . . ." "Say it, Doc," said the voyager. "Stumps." The premise was that now the voyager *felt* things through prosthetic limbs with a different kind of sensibility. Sight, touch, sound, smell, taste—nothing felt the same, and it certainly meant something different.

Periodically people ask me about my "divided" life, apparently in reference not only to my continual geographic or even cultural displacement (I have returned to Brazil many times over the years, living in both Rio de Janeiro and Salvador, Bahia) but also to my simultaneous professional study of literary theory and Afro-Brazilian dance. Although I consequently have become very interested in questions of ethnography, I never intended to be an anthropologist. In fact, while I deeply love *Tristes tropiques,* the melancholia that pervades the book makes one marvel that anyone could choose a profession of such profound alienation and repeated loss.[2] My own choice to live in Brazil has at times felt to me like a choice to be happy, at other times like a self-wounding. But my intention was never to do fieldwork.

The divided life to which people refer is not just geographic, nor the doubled alienation of the participant-observer. What they perceive as division is rather (and it is often articulated in exactly this way) that of "having both a mind and a body"—that is, being both an intellectual and a dancer. Of course the irony is implicit in the figuration. Mind and body would seem to create a totality, a wholeness to a life. But intellectuals in the United States know that the *corpus sanus mens sana* engraved over a university gymnasium door is no indication of a developed understanding of the place of the body in the process of intellectualization.

To be sure, literary theorists have broached the issue. But whether language and thought are theorized as bodily phenomena[3] or theory itself is figured as a "fleshly" endeavor,[4] one would be hard pressed to articulate these notions in bodily motion. In this country, dance scholarship has tended to be less than flexible. Even in the rare and specific contexts in which the body's motion is acknowledged to be communicating something, we have a limited notion of what the communication comprises. Most U.S. dance scholars have an understanding of the meaning of dance that still fundamentally assumes a mind-body division. Significance is ascribed to the choreographic act: the art of designed motion. In Brazil, there are certain dances which, in effect, write their own meanings. And there is an understanding of the possibility of a corporeal intelligence. There are things I learned in Brazil with my body, and some of these things it has taken me years to learn to articulate in writing. But that is not to say that they were without meaning when I could only speak them through dance.

The division I myself have felt over these years has not been a separation of mind and body, or of mind or body from home (the amputated man!). It has been, rather, the distance between ways of articulating knowledge in two diverse intellectual communities. In Afro-Brazilian culture, dance is acknowledged as a significant cultural activity. Those who possess a superior knowledge of dance forms are seen as repositories of tradition and as scholars. As in the Western academy, their scholarly prestige may be determined by a combination of a grasp of the tradition, an ability to interpret or theorize it, and a personal capacity for innovation.

U.S. scholars of modern or classical dance sometimes ask me about my interests in choreography. The word itself needs to be reconsidered in the context of traditional or folkloric dance. Authorial innovation means something quite different when the origins of certain dances are attributed to divine sources or when "faithful" rendering of a traditional style might indicate political affiliations. That is not to say that Western-style choreographies are not being created by Brazilian dancers. I studied Afro-Brazilian dance at the Federal University of Bahia. The dance department is, in fact, one of its most respected departments. Young dance scholars there are developing technical and pedagogical methods derived from the traditions they teach, as opposed to the technical exercises from ballet and modern traditions which were formerly held to constitute basic training for all dancers.[5] Dance technique is understood by these dancers as an integral part of the lives of bodies in the communities that have produced dance traditions. Their exercises draw on Afro-Brazilian postures and gestures, from the quotidian to the highly ritual. But these scholars are also choreographing, in styles which reflect the interaction of Western, African, and indigenous forms and their underlying philosophies. Such an interaction is not surprising in the cosmopolitan, urban setting of Bahia.

The choreographers like to distinguish between categories of dance, such as folkloric, spontaneous, and professional. But in fact, all forms of dance are constantly absorbing influences, old and new.

The cosmopolitanism of Bahia is evidenced not just by international tourism, by the Club Med on the island off the shore, or by the influx of Western styles and moves. Bahia is also a community with a heightened cosmopolitanism in the sense that the anthropologist Paul Rabinow has defined the term: "an ethos of macro-interdependencies, with an acute consciousness (often forced upon people) of the inescapabilities and particularities of places, characters, historical trajectories, and fates."[6] Rabinow suggests that this is the ethos of the postmodern ethnographer, and yet he implies that it is a consciousness ("often forced upon people") which has preceded the ethnographer to postcolonial communities. And while certainly contemporary Brazil is a place of strange contiguities and cultural self-irony, it is questionable whether this is strictly a postmodern or even postcolonial phenomenon. In fact, some would argue that cultural self-consciousness and revision were the norm in African cultures even before they were transplanted to Brazil.

Margaret Thompson Drewal has analyzed traditional Yoruba ritual dance in Nigeria[7] and its syncretic offshoots in Brazil. Yoruba performers in Nigeria describe themselves as people of action, as *aṣe* (written *axé* in Brazil). Drewal cites improvisation and spontaneity as the continually self-destabilizing foundation of a cultural tradition. And certainly by Yoruba accounts, *aşe* preceded the cultural contiguities of colonialism and the slave trade. Prior to both these phenomena, Yoruba culture was urban, active, and spontaneous; it valued innovation. In this sense, the innovative young dance scholars in Bahia are working precisely in a Yoruba tradition, as are the kids on the street who create, absorb, transform, and syncretize dance forms on a daily basis.

I studied dance at the university, but I have also studied in other contexts not generally perceived, at least in the United States, as academic. And I learned as much about pedagogy and intellectualism as I did about dance. The houses of traditional Afro-Brazilian religious worship are filled with dance. In fact, worship cannot take place, cannot be meaningful, without dance. The women and men who instruct young people in the dances of the gods are passing on tremendously significant knowledge. Witnessing this kind of cultural transmission has deepened my sense of what it can mean to teach. The pedagogy of religious dance is a passing on of forms, but it becomes meaningful when it embodies belief. I myself have come to believe that all teaching becomes meaningful when it acknowledges its ground of belief—which may not be articulated as spiritual but rather as political or even aesthetic. Acknowledgment of belief need not be restrictive or dogmatic. It may rather open out a field of possible significance.

In the "academies" of *capoeira*, a traditionally politicized Afro-Brazilian dance/martial art, masters continually remind students of the historical significance of what they are learning. As they go through the motions of capoeira, they are also embodying a historical racial struggle. This literal embodiment of a tradition is perhaps the most important lesson.

When one begins to learn through unfamiliar pedagogies and acknowledges other forms of intellectualism, one's own intellectual training comes into question. How sensible or useful is it to translate between Western and non-Western theoretical models? This issue has come under particularly intense debate in African diasporic studies in recent years. Paulin Hountondji has urged African scholars to develop a philosophical dialogue independent of European discussions.[8] And in African American literary studies, Henry Louis Gates, Jr., in *The Signifying Monkey*, has set as his goal "to allow the black tradition to speak for itself about its nature and various functions, rather than to read it, or analyze it, in terms of literary theories borrowed whole from other traditions, appropriated from without."[9] The challenge to find an indigenous theoretical system in diasporic culture is a strong and compelling one. But the scholar who finds herself straddling intellectual traditions will inevitably do a certain amount of translation. It goes both ways.

My own sense is that a hungry mind will eat off of diverse plates. It could be argued that Gates's signifying monkey, the Yoruba trickster-god Eṣu, bears an uncanny resemblance to a certain tricky French theorist. But is that appropriation? Many times in Brazil I've gotten into a political or aesthetic or even personal discussion and been told that my premise—which I considered theoretical—was the *orixá* (divine master) of my head talking. I was just mouthing for the divinity.

SAMBA

By the same token, I've found myself recounting to friends in the United States some of my experiences with the orixás and heard them respond, "So, in psychoanalytic terms, what you're saying is . . ." Both responses are reductive only if one considers the theoretical system by which they operate reductive. But one could also see them as expansive.

That brings me back to the issue of belief. To speak from a theoretical system is to subscribe to it on some level. In this book, I position myself within various systems, but probably that which will seem strangest to readers in the United States will be the belief system of Afro-Brazilian religion—the *candomblé*. I have found the question of my own beliefs to be the one most often raised in discussions of my work. People are concerned about "objectivity" when not only ritual participation but also subscription is at stake. Maya Deren, in *Divine Horsemen,* raises a similar question in a footnote in reference to her own "possession" by a Haitian goddess:

> Since the loa mounted my head, is this to say that I believe in Voudoun and in Erzulie? In the context of Voudoun, such a question did not occur to me. I would say that, as a metaphysical and ritualistic structure Voudoun *is a fact,* and does exist, and that, as such, it incorporates values with which I am in personal agreement, displays an organizational, psychic and practical skill which I admire, and accomplishes results of which I approve. I believe that the principles which Ghede and the other loa represent are real and true, in the sense that it is true, for instance, that nature follows a

life-death-life cycle; and the possessions which I have
witnessed have seemed to me to be exemplary and
absolute personifications of these principles. It was this
kind of agreement with, and admiration for the
principles and practices of Voudoun which was and is my
conscious attitude towards it. Otherwise I simply
participated in it to the extent that an average serviteur
might, and with the average proportion of pleasure,
boredom, and discomfort, according to the
circumstances. I observed the appropriate conventions
and formalities of the rituals which I attended, sang the
songs as I became familiar with them, and danced the
dances. In effect, and regardless of what I might think or
believe, I *served* the loa and, in so doing, I learned . . .
that the effect of the ritual service is upon the doer.[10]

Deren sidesteps the question of belief by arguing that
her experiences are like those of "an average serviteur,"
like any Haitian who, as part of the culture, is not called
upon to explain its beliefs. Participation is a matter of
going through the motions, but going through the motions has effect "upon the doer."

More recently, Karen McCarthy Brown has repeated Deren's sidestep. Also writing of her participation in Haitian religious ceremonies, she argues that
service to the loa is based on pragmatism. But in this
respect she says her experiences in the religion "both
are and are not like those of Haitians."[11] As she is a
U.S. student of the religion, the pragmatic purpose of
her participation may at times be personal, but it is also
academic.

I believe both Deren and Brown. Deren's observation that the average "believer"[12] attends to worship by

going through the motions does not preclude her or
him from experiencing both exultation and pain. More
interesting, the act of singing the songs and dancing
the dances can clarify the kinds of belief which we find
easier to articulate—what Deren calls values, skill, and
principles. But Brown's concession is no doubt also
true. When an outsider chooses to go through another
culture's motions, she may believe hotly in her actions,
but the possibility of translating them means they "are
and are not" the same. The possibility of translation divides experience. And yet the act is what one hopes
will heal it. My purpose in writing about the dances is
to try to heal the body divided from its intellect—to
hook up neural connections to these false but painfully
sensitive limbs I seem to have acquired in an unlikely
accident. Of course I said the rift was a perceived one,
and doesn't actually apply in a culture which comprehends intelligent bodies. But what of my own culture?
And it isn't at all inappropriate to bring the metaphor
of physical violence into a discussion of African culture
in Brazil. This is a cultural tradition that has suffered the
continual threat of literal corporal punishment for practitioners, as well as the figural violence against a body
of cultural knowledge. Slavery brought specific, real
pain to the bodies of women and men, and misapprehension of cultural practices, including in an international context, continues to threaten tradition.

The question of *how* to write about these dances is
complex. I have said I am interested in the problems of
ethnography—but that is not to say I have arrived at a

singular solution. My training is in literary analysis, not anthropology. But the disciplines are increasingly entangled. Not only are more literary critics turning to cultural analysis (usually of their own, avoiding the discomfort of fieldwork), but ethnographers are turning to literature to understand their own project. Of course, over forty years ago, structuralism offered an analytic methodology to linguists, anthropologists, and literary critics alike. But poststructural critics consider not only the methods but also the thematics of anthropology, and ethnographers have begun to examine the literary aspects of their own work. The constitution of ethnographic authority is seen, more and more, as a question of authorship.

Still, critical ethnographers hold to the value of their own fieldwork. This isn't just the swaggering of adventurers (although an element of this may be present). It is a theoretical commitment to the fact, as James Clifford puts it, that "participant observation obliges its practitioners to experience, at a bodily as well as an intellectual level, the vicissitudes of translation."[13] Clifford argues that while fieldwork may not always achieve its ideals, it does demand a certain degree of self-consciousness and a willingness to be culturally displaced. Furthermore, he suggests that the practice of fieldwork need not only be associated with Western anthropology as a totalizing or reductive discipline, since interdisciplinary methodological exchanges are taking place. This book counts itself as part of this project of exchange.

The interdisciplinary project proposed by Clifford and his colleagues is not without its critics. Lila Abu-Lughod eyed with suspicion the landmark collection of essays edited by Clifford and George Marcus, *Writing Culture,*[14] not only because of its paucity of female contributors but also because of its "hyper-professionalism." The essays, she writes, draw on "elite disciplines like philosophy and literary studies," not on "more prosaic sources like ordinary experience."[15] Ordinary experience sounds more modest than fieldwork, and it is a phrase which calls to mind human interaction rather than an arduous, possibly dangerous journey and physical conditions. Abu-Lughod recounts a tradition—neglected by recent "experimental" ethnographers—of women writing alternative forms of cultural analysis. These are the "non-professional," largely anecdotal accounts of Western women (often accompanying their husbands) who find themselves in unfamiliar places. Abu-Lughod relates these works to those of "halfies," writers of mixed ethnic background who translate their own experiences in another challenge to standard ethnographic authority. A feminist ethnography, according to Abu-Lughod, would acknowledge and validate the anecdotal, the "non-professional," and the "non-objective," as all-inclusiveness, professionalism, and objectivity are the very doctrines of normative anthropology which have effaced women's and non-Western perspectives.

I strongly agree with Abu-Lughod's proposals regarding anecdote and personal experience, as will become clear in the following chapters. But what of her disdain for the "elite discipline" of literary studies, and my own references to it? The cultural traditions I examine here are extraordinarily complex and sophisticated. I have drawn on various resources to grapple with them. If some of the theoretical terminology or maneuvers seem difficult, this is by no means due to a desire for intellectual elitism, nor a desire to discipline or control the dances. On the contrary, I want to open out a space for the dances' significance to resonate. The connections I make are arbitrary, personal, and, I hope, instructive.

Brazilian dance offers entirely different ways of thinking about language, writing, representation, narrative, even irony. This means not only that I have been drawn to describe dance in literary terms but also that I find myself examining my own ways of writing about it. Aside from the political arguments for anecdotal cultural analysis, it has seemed to me that personal anecdote is a manner of putting you, a reader, through my own steps, both physical and intellectual. But anecdote can't quite tell the whole story. This is a history without closure, and individual stories seem to dissolve into strange, dispersed lyrical moments. The samba itself is both a story and a poem. And this may be why it fascinates me. When I was living in Brazil I was writing poetry, but poems that were weighed down with political frustration at the same time that they wanted to lift off the page with a sense I think was exultation. I was maddened and awed by my neighbors' insistence on living the stereotype of the adamantly celebratory Brazilian. The community that maintains these dances is always hungry. It lives spotted across urban areas on

SAMBA

hills called *favelas,* which are shantytowns. I lived on a favela called Mermaid Hill in Salvador, Bahia, the heart of African Brazil. We looked across a gaping avenue at another favela, the Hill of Happiness, where numerous samba competitions took place. You could hear them as night fell on the Hill of Happiness creating a racket to keep despair at bay.

Despite all pressures, the culture is resilient. It certainly doesn't need my writing to preserve it. Brazilians have other forms of cultural record keeping—and dance is one. Although the religious and popular dances are not choreographed in the Western sense, they are themselves a kind of bodily writing. These dances are the texts I read here. The text I produce, then, in an attempt to incorporate some of the lessons of the dances, will necessarily be self-reflexive. Acknowledging dance as a form of cultural inscription means I have to ask myself—why write?

For a time, while I lived in Brazil, I stopped writing. I learned to dance. I also learned to pray and fight—two things I had never before felt called upon to do. I did them with my body. I began to think with my body. That is possible and, in the case of Brazilian dance, necessary. What I write here, in words, cannot contain the significance of the dances. I only mean to indicate the ground of their meaningfulness.

This is the figure to which I find myself returning. I am writing to find a ground—of belief, and of meaning. Writing as a ground reminds me of the kind of inscription of dance we associate with Arthur Murray and the ballroom styles, those funny, indecipherable maps of footprints.

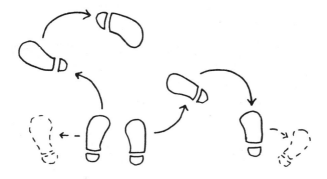

It looks ridiculous—and yet if the dances could really impress themselves like that, like the prints of their own significance on the page, there would be no need to translate. If ethnography were only so simple!

My understanding of the significance of writing has been informed by dance—and vice versa. The chapters that follow map certain principles we generally ascribe to literature as they direct or ground specific dances. In the first chapter, I read the samba—the most popular secular dance in Brazil—as a form that narrates a history of cultural contact between Africans, Europeans, and indigenous Brazilians. This story, however, is not acted out mimetically but is compressed in a single musical phrase. It is precisely the kind of narrative compression into lyrical moments which I have suggested occurs in the narration of a history without closure—samba as both story and poem.

The second chapter, on the dances of the candomblé, the African religious ceremonies in Brazil, examines a question I have already raised here: what constitutes choreography when the design of motion is ascribed to divine sources? The candomblé dances are understood to be embodiments not of the expressive potential of individual dancers but rather of the principles of belief which bind a community together. The dances, in fact, rewrite the significance (including the sexed and sexualized significance) of the bodies that actualize them. This understanding of authorship has necessarily made me reflect on my own desires to write about the dances. My sense is that I can only write significantly about the candomblé choreographies to the degree that I myself write in service of the principles that make them meaningful.

The third chapter looks at capoeira, the dance which embodies a history of racial struggle. Capoeira is both fascinating and elusive. The difficulty of fixing it in descriptive writing is that capoeira's strategy is one of constant motion—both literal and figurative. Just as we ascribe a straightforward meaning to it, we find it is turning itself upside down with self-irony. The physical inversions are redoubled—or set spinning—by the figural inversions on which they are grounded.

Finally, the fourth chapter looks to the Bahian *carnaval* as a closing scene where all of the dance forms are set out in spectacle. But carnaval can never serve for narrative closure, because it is the place where all boundaries—including narrative—explode.

Throughout these analyses, the boundaries between specific dance forms seem to disintegrate. In textual terms, the body in Afro-Brazilian dance continually cites itself. Gestures from religious and martial dance resonate in the secular samba—and samba infiltrates the circles of candomblé and capoeira. Another way of putting it would be to say that in a seemingly purely aesthetic moment, there are spiritual and political references. But spirituality in African Brazil doesn't exclude notions of politics or aesthetics—or even, for that matter, of sexuality. This quality, the one which informs U.S. stereotypes regarding Brazilian dance, is more complicated than it may seem. In fact, preconceptions, stereotypes applied from abroad, have been absorbed into the dances themselves. They may be ironized, or played out on a mimetic level. In any case, North Americans, even from an uninformed position, are already implicated in the dances.

If I could make you understand these multiple levels of meaning in the body dancing samba, I would have written with the grace of the *bamba,* the expert sambista. Teaching, not long ago, a class in recent literary theory, it struck me that what I was doing was remarkably similar—and nearly as difficult—as teaching samba. Literary theorists in the past two decades have located the ground on which we establish significance. Then we pulled the rug out from under our feet and showed that it was merely a structure, then pulled the structure out from under that. We have been doing a very fancy dance ever since in an effort to keep from falling down meaningless. These levels of trip-steps and feints are as difficult to keep going as the three separate rhythms articulated in the feet, hips, and shoulders of the sambista. But of course we never *really* wanted to lose a ground of significance. We just wanted a more naked truth: down to the G-string of meaning! Myself, I have no problem with exhibitionism.

But what about the sambista—would she turn the comparison around—and would she desire this much significance? More. Certainly she wouldn't say it this way. She would be more eloquent. But she'd be just as overfigurative, gawdy, and self-conscious.

1. Samba: The Body Articulate

Samba is the dance of the body articulate. What does it mean to speak with the body? In Portuguese, one says that the skilled sambista is able, and obliged, to "dizer no pé"—speak with the feet.[1] No other language is required: song is redundant, words are superfluous. You recognize this in the Rio carnaval: there is an eloquence in the white shoes, in the silver high heels scraping the asphalt. You can see it daily in the familiar shantytowns pocking the hills around white moneyed neighborhoods, in the bare feet stamping down on a concrete floor. In the samba, in fact, not only the feet speak. The dance is a complex dialogue in which various parts of the body talk at the same time, and in seemingly different languages. The feet keep up a rapid patter, while the hips beat out a heavy staccato and the shoulders roll a slow drawl. It is all funky with message. To articulate means, of course, to flex at the joints, and samba may seem fluid and jointless, and at the same time entirely disjointed. The message is simultaneously narrative and lyrical. That is to say, it spins itself out over time, increasing in meaning as it recounts its origins; and yet it compresses its significance in a momentary image. Samba narrates a story of racial contact, conflict, and resistance, not just mimetically across a span of musical time but also synchronically, in the depth of a single measure.

When we speak of narration, we assume an element of linearity.[2] A story—or history—takes place in, and over, a span of time. Our telling of it, similarly, takes place over time. But the sequence of events, be they real or fictional, doesn't necessarily correspond to the sequence of their telling. Analysts of narrative distinguish between the two time lines and assign significance not only to those events recounted (and—perhaps particularly—those unrecounted) but also to the divergence in their order. In musical terms, one might describe such divergence as polymeter—the layering of rhythmic times. In narrative terms, this is diachrony, and it is what complicates all accounts of historical events, such as the colonization of Brazil, the suppression of indigenous peoples and cultures, and the period of the enslavement of African peoples, which lasted longer in Brazil than in any other nation in the New World. The preceding sentence is, itself, a kind of supercompressed narrative, which could use some spinning out here.

The Portuguese began importing African slaves to Brazil in the mid-sixteenth century. The first antislave commerce legislation was enacted in 1831, but to little avail. In 1871, the rule of *ventre libre* ("free womb") was approved, promising free status to the children of enslaved women. It was not until the *Lei Aurea* (Golden Law) of 1888 that abolition took place—officially. Black Brazilians, however, frequently refer to that date as the inception of a "falsa abolição," when Afro-Brazilians merely shifted from one kind of slave quarters to another: the favelas. Historical documents—including records of the importation of Africans—were destroyed at the time of abolition in a gesture which was intended by the governing class, they said, to erase the shame of slavery.[3] Of course the destruction of the text could not abolish the story. It is important not only to recover that lost narrative but also to understand the story as it persists in the present.

The physical destruction of historical records is not the only gap in the narrative of the history of blacks in Brazil. Social histories have been notoriously reticent about the hardships inflicted upon nonwhites. In this country, the sociologist Thomas Skidmore has spent two decades calling into question the popular myth of Brazilian racial equity.[4] Given the economic destitution of the vast majority of blacks and the virtual absence of major political figures of color in Brazil, it is perhaps hard to fathom the durability of the myth of equity. But

SAMBA

Brazil—Bahia in particular—seems to represent, even to many blacks from the United States, a kind of mecca of African-New World cultural pride. Much of it has to do with the personal, quotidian relations between the races. For tourists from the United States, it's a stunning experience to step into an atmosphere where racial tension appears not only not to exist but in fact to have been replaced by a love-fest of things black on the part of middle-class whites. Discrimination exists, one is told, but it is on the basis of class, not race.

So why are all the blacks so terribly poor? The Brazilian establishment is ready to concede to class discrimination. But race has effectively been erased as a term from discussions of postabolition society, up to the very present. Erasure is precisely the word here, because it is the metaphor behind the ideology of color which has led to these accounts full of holes. From early on in this century, social theorists have suggested that mixed-race Brazilian society was undergoing a continual process of "whitening": miscegenation was thinning out the black population, while European immigration was reinforcing the trend toward whiteness. Early arguments of this type explicitly suggested that such a trend was favorable, given the innate "superiority" of the white race (the most famous proponent of this theory was, interestingly, the mixed-race writer Oliveira Vianna).[5] In the 1930s, Gilberto Freyre countered the explicitly racist theory of whitening with a seemingly more benign version. Freyre agreed that the trend was toward whiteness ("Negroes are now rapidly disappearing in Brazil, merging into the white stock").[6] But his interpretation of the significance of miscegenation was pointedly contrary to Vianna's. Freyre prophesied a "new world in the tropics," a society populated by the culturally enriched products of racial mixing. Freyre studied anthropology with Franz Boas, whom he credited with having opened his eyes to the economic determinants of social status. Freyre's counterargument to Vianna was that if black and mixed-race Brazilians appeared to be a "mongrel" lot, it was due to their economic oppression, not to white racial "superiority." In fact, according to Freyre, contact with non-Europeans in Brazil was only bettering white culture:

> the development of a modern civilization in Brazil is becoming more and more the development of a new type of civilization. . . . More than any other people, they are developing a modern civilization in the tropics whose predominant traits are European, but whose perspectives—I should insist on this point—are extra-European.[7]

Freyre's racially mixed Brazil was a brave new world, enhanced by its cultural diversity. When Freyre first proposed his theories, they were viewed as progressive and clearly antiracist. But in the decades that followed, they were taken up by a governing class which was all too eager to obfuscate questions of racial inequity. As Skidmore has argued, Freyre set out to attack Vianna, yet ironically he "reinforce[d] the whitening ideal by showing graphically that the (primarily white) elite had gained valuable cultural traits from their intimate contact with the African (and Indian, to a lesser extent)."[8] The very fact of Freyre's progressive origins has obscured the reactionary uses to which his writings have been put. But by the 1960s, vocal intellectuals (a group destined for censorship and forced exile by the military regime) were attacking Freyre as "inevitably dated and anachronistic."[9]

That Freyre's position was (and is) dated seems painfully evident to us. Certain Brazilian intellectuals may have abandoned him, and yet his ideas have tremendous currency among the population at large. It was Freyre who formulated the supposed existence of a "Brazilian racial democracy" which is so dear to unpoliticized blacks and whites alike. He extended the humanistic principle that it is poverty, not racial inferiority, that degenerates men, and argued that in Brazil, consequently, discrimination falls along economic, not color, lines: "There has been, and still is, social distance between different groups of the population. But social distance is . . . the result of class consciousness rather than of race or color prejudice."[10] Recent reevaluations of the argument by Brazilian social theorists range from the ambivalent to the indignant. Oracy Nogueira writes that "Brazilian racial democracy" is a "negative" term, as it is a misrepresentation of the facts, but is "positive" as a social ideal.[11] Carlos Hasenbalg goes further, insisting that the racial democracy myth is part of "a wider matrix of ideological conservatism where the preservation of national unity and social peace are the paramount concerns."[12] Hasenbalg's most provocative point—and he is dead right—is that the term's primary function is to exclude the mention of race from political discussion.

The erasure of race from Brazil's political history has been remarkably continuous—from the ostensibly humanistic destruction of slavery documents through the ostensibly humanistic avowal of racial democracy.

As Skidmore has noted, "between 1890 and 1940 neither the Brazilian government nor Brazilian social scientists considered race to be a significant enough variable to justify recording it in the national census."[13] Until 1976, in fact, no one bothered to correlate data on social status (income, education, health, etc.) and race. And when race is invoked by the government, it continues to be in the same wishful platitudes that Freyre offered up in the 1930s. The most recent constitution, drafted in 1988, declared racism illegal. But nuts-and-bolts legislation hasn't followed, and the principle itself is practically unenforceable. For radicals like Abdías do Nascimento, there is an especially cruel irony to this situation. In 1945, he and several others drafted a manifesto calling for the illegalization of racism.[14] Forty-three years later, they got it, in the form of "Problem? What problem?" from the government. Florestan Fernandes, another outspoken critic of the status quo, has most succinctly defined the problem: Brazil has "the prejudice of having no prejudice."[15]

It's such a tricky state of affairs, one can begin to understand the reluctance of many blacks to declare their opposition to a government which professes to be constitutionally antiracist. But since the 1970s, there has been a steady tide of resistance rising among young blacks who got the big picture. They've been telling each other another story. Popular accounts of race relations in Brazil, which hold that abolition never took place in a meaningful way (a "false abolition" leading to the favela as modern slaves' quarters), are grounded in historical and demographic realities. It might be argued that they operate on a figural level, as slavery is no longer literally, legislatively, a reality. But the insidiousness of these word games is all too apparent. The stunning poverty and virtually complete economic dependence of black Brazilians is hardly a metaphor. And yet the poor black tenant of a favela employed as a domestic servant who calls herself a slave is aware of the power of the word, and of her own articulateness in saying it. She reads herself in relation to her African antecedent as both a representation of a woman erased from Brazilian history and a continuation of the same woman's story. I do not mean to diminish the power of this gesture by suggesting it is lyrical as well as narrative. This is a strong lyricism grounded in racial identification. These are the bare feet stamping down on a concrete floor. A person can say these things in so many words. Or a person can speak with the body.

The lyricism of the samba is its incorporation of figures that flash across time. Dance ethnography has often referred to such figures as African or indigenous "survivals"—gestures in contemporary dances that can be traced or inferred to preslavery and precolonial sources. The term *survival* acknowledges the fact of cultural repression, but it fails to recognize that African and indigenous culture in the New World has not merely held on but has grown and developed subsequent to the moment of historical rupture. In the case of Brazil, backward-looking projects of inference are often confounded by the lack of textual sources. We have the nineteenth-century engravings of Debret, Rugendas, and Martius and Spix, which show freeze-frame gestures and dance configurations. We have spotty written depictions of indigenous dances of Brazil and West Africa at the point of first contact with Europeans, although these are written from the perspective of viewers completely unfamiliar with the rhythmic and gestural vocabularies they attempt to describe. Examining contemporary dances of relatively isolated indigenous communities in Brazil and Africa is a shot in the dark. A direct comparison of these dances with the samba would not take into account the contemporaneous modifications which have taken place over centuries in these communities. Dance ethnography can never be convincing historiography.[16] Rhythmic and gestural vocabulary—the language of the body—can endure, but it is not merely frozen in time. It can itself refer to ruptures in historical time, rhythmic disjunction—and it can figure itself in relation to its past, as the *favelada* figures herself in relation to her ancestor. It doesn't mean they do the same dance. Even if the gestures are the same, they have accrued a double, self-reflexive significance. My project here is to locate the space between a narrative and a figural reading of Brazilian dance. This is neither a purely historical nor a purely semiotic analysis.[17] I mean, rather, to allow for a synthesis of time and signs, which would be the only way to account for the complex speaking of the body in Brazil.

The body says what cannot be spoken. Musically, this can be explained as syncopation. Samba is a polymeter, layered over a 2/4 structure. But the strong beat is suspended, the weak accentuated. This suspension leaves the body with a hunger that can only be satisfied

SAMBA

by filling the silence with motion. Samba, the dance, cannot exist without the suppression of a strong beat. Polymeter is a manner of describing rhythmic structures which combine various ways of counting. It is the dominant mode of all pan-African music, and it is what distinguishes this music from Western forms in which harmonic and melodic progression predominate. A person schooled in the European musical tradition may, on encountering a polymeter, find it incomprehensibly complex or may apprehend a surface texture which seems not to *go* anywhere—hence the complaint of monotony. The problem is, in a sense, not the indirection of the music but the misdirection of the listening. The interest of harmonic-melodic music is in its pattern across time: the way the line varies or chords progress. The interest of polymetric music is in the simultaneous patterns which are established in a single measure. One reads Western music, on the page, from left to right. If polymetric music is notated, one must read it vertically in order to perceive its complexity. This is not to say that it doesn't change over time. In fact, the breaks in rhythmic structure, the ruptures in the pattern, are the points at which the full complexity of the original pattern becomes evident. But the break precisely points out all that was inherent or potential in the texture before the tear.

Western musical notation is by no means adequate for inscribing polymeters. Samba cannot be convincingly programmed into a computerized drum machine, as it contains rhythms bent so slightly that their variation can't be broken down even into sixty-fourths. But an inaccurate inscription is perhaps the only way to represent here the exigencies of reading the rhythm synchronically—up and down. The basic texture of samba requires that these patterns be in place:

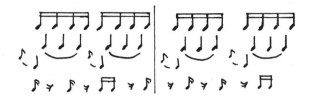

These two bars represent the basic phrase. In the first, two strong beats are established. In the second, these beats are suspended in the *clave* part, the final line in this notation. *Clave* is Spanish for "key," and it is the term generally used to refer to the rhythmic pattern which is fundamental to any polymeter. In a sense it is analogous to the European notion of a clef or key which organizes harmonic relations. The clave is a regular irregularity. For those unfamiliar with polymeters, it is generally the part most difficult to make heads or tails of. It appears arbitrary, seems to come in and out of rhythm. In order to play it, one must let go of the downbeat. The clave in its capriciousness assumes a quality which seems melodic. It is, effectively, the *song* of any polymeter. And it is the key, in the sense that it opens all the other patterns which might otherwise appear locked. The clave of the samba breaks the count of one-x-two-x-one-x-two into one-two-xx-one-two-three-xx. This three-count brings into relief the tighter, rapid triplets of the second line of the notation. These are not, in fact, true triplets, as one beat is slightly weighted—generally, the second of each set. The bottom-heavy

SAMBA

center triplet sets the strong beat off balance—an imbalance recomplicated by the clave's trip-step.

The basic samba step appears to articulate the triplets. It requires levity, speed, and dexterity; it also requires accuracy, but not in the sense of hitting the rhythm on the mark. It must locate itself *between* rhythms. The dance is on a three-count—right-left-right/left-right-left—but it also weights one count, either the first or the second triplet. It may accentuate or contradict the weighting of the triplets in the music. As one triplet is heavier, the step slides toward the first line of rapid sixteenth-notes. The stronger step gives almost two sixteenths to itself and hints at that doubleness by, in an instant, shifting the weight from the ball of the foot to the heel: a double articulation or flexing at the joint. The step is *between* a triplet set and four sixteenth-notes. The relation between the feet and the rhythm might be approximately notated as:

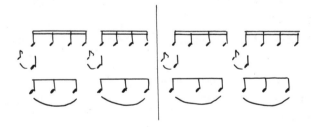

b-h   b   b   b-h   b   b   b-h   b   b   b-h   b   b

On each step marked b-h (ball-heel), the weight of the body is pitched slightly forward, while the next two steps (ball-ball) are a mere lifting up and back in preparation for the next pitch forward. The dance that I have inscribed here is a simple version in which the pitching forward occurs on the initial beat. A funkier version of the step would pitch forward rather on the second beat of each set of triplets. That is a recomplication of the rhythm which most Western students find somewhat more difficult, although it is merely a resituation of the same step within the rhythmic structure—another dislocation of the downbeat.

If you are reading this in an attempt to learn the dance, this is the moment at which you will shake your head in exasperation. It will only make things worse if I tell you that while this is happening, the hips—particularly if you are a woman—must lag slightly behind the feet so that their triplet, while it follows the same right-left-right pattern, will accentuate or weight a beat slightly after that of the feet, while your shoulders (strange quietude over this cacophony) will simply roll on the one and two of the third line of my original notation. I have taught Brazilian dance for years, and if ever I had prefaced a class with this description I would have lost even the most agile of my students. Western students of polymetric music and dance often request that the rhythms be broken down, but a complete breakdown results in just that—the rhythm breaks down. Our frequent admonition—stop thinking and dance—isn't to say that the motion is unthinkable. It's to say that the body is capable of understanding more things at once than can be articulated in language. One has no choice but to *think with the body*.

The dancer may be able to accommodate more simultaneous rhythms than the individual musicians in a samba ensemble. Robert Farris Thompson coined the phrase "apart-playing" to describe the way in which the individual musicians work together to create a polymeter.[18] Each player concentrates on his part (I use the masculine pronoun here as it most realistically represents the gender of the players in most Brazilian percussive groups), and the separate lines of thought coincide at the beginning of each phrase. But the *meaning* of these separate lines only becomes apparent when they come together. The dancer may make reference to all of them with different parts of her body. This is a synthetic quality of pan-African dance generally. John Miller Chernoff has noted that African drummers say they *understand* a polymeter by knowing how to dance it: "In African music, it is the listener or dancer who has to supply the beat: the listener must be *actively engaged* in making sense of the music."[19] When one watches a sambista dance, one is watching a gesture of making significance.

I said that samba is layered over a 2/4 structure. In the notation, this fundamental beat can be read in the third line. In the instrumentation of a modern samba band, the fundamental 2/4 beat is played by an instrument called the *surdo*. The surdo is an enormous bass drum which is strapped over the shoulder. *Surdo* means "deaf" in Portuguese. It can be understood as referring to the effect of the deep pounding on the player or the listener. But it might also be understood as the quality of sound produced by the drum. The surdo is so extremely deep in tone, so very bass, that its effect is like a negative utterance. It seems in a sense to erase or negate that moment in sound. Samba as a rhythm not only suspends its downbeat through the clave, but even in its stressing of this beat it blacks it out. The accompanying dance can fill the gap with a strong step or can reinforce its dislocation with another kind of suspension. But marking the absence of the downbeat is another way of indicating it. However the samba is danced, *it is the suspension or silencing of a beat which provokes movement.*

The same can be said of samba historically. Samba is a dance that generally attracts attention for its frenetic exuberance. It is regarded as a secular form, neither religious nor overtly political. It is also known as the Brazilian national dance and has contributed to a world image of Brazil as a country of exaggerated elation, in which joyous movement is considered meaningful in and of itself. But samba means more than this. And if its steps can only be called forth by syncopation, its deeper meanings can only be evoked by another kind of suppression, which is racial, cultural, and political. Those who would promote samba as a purely aesthetic form, the Brazilian national dance in its most harmless sense, are also those who have long promoted the fiction of a Brazilian racial democracy—a fiction which began to be inscribed with the destruction of the documents of slavery. This is another form of negative articulation, an erasure of a historical moment which in fact brings this moment into relief. This fiction has silenced a history of cultural and political repression of blacks and indigenous peoples. Samba speaks this history.

I said that samba narrates racial contact synchronically, not across time like most fictions or histories. But there is a fiction sometimes used to explain the history of samba—"a história do negro e da índia," the story of the black man and the "Indian" woman. (I use here and elsewhere the term *Indian*, as opposed to indigenous Brazilian, to refer not to a literal and culturally significant people but rather to the highly figurative image constructed by colonists and appropriated and ironized by the blacks in Brazil, as will be discussed below.) The story goes that in the early days of colonization, an escaped black slave encountered a *cabocla*—an Indian woman—in the bush. As both were sick and tired of life among the Portuguese, they chose to set up housekeeping there in the wild, and their children began a *mestiço* race. The only difficulty was the parents' inability to communicate in each other's language, so their arguments took place in stomps, shakes, and shudders: the samba. The word (of uncertain origin) *zamba* means a mestiço child, offspring of an African father and an indigenous mother. But few ethnologists suppose that this is the real source of the term *samba* as it refers to a particular rhythm and style of dance. This narrative of the birth of samba is obviously fictional, but it serves precisely to illustrate to what degree the encounter between Africans and indigenous Brazilians has had to be fictionalized by white society in order to diminish its political potential. The identification of the two races in their resistance against whites was and is threatening. The reduction of the encounter to a benign love story culminating in samba is a manner of defusing the threat. But ironically, it is samba which tells the story left silent in the fictional version.

If *zamba* is not the source of the term, what is? I will begin with one of the less popular hypotheses.

Baptista Siqueira notes that in the seventeenth century, Jesuit missionaries recorded the term *samba* among the Cariri people of Brazil in reference to a kind of wild tortoise which was a delicacy served at festive gatherings. The meaning of the word later expanded to signify the physical space of communal festivities. Siqueira cites a journalistic account from the turn of the century that seems to incorporate the Cariri in a fictional construct that resembles the story we've already heard:

> the dance is a function of dances: the samba is a mixture of the *jongo* of the African percussive ensembles, of the Sugarcane dance of the Portuguese and of the *poracé* of the Indians. The three races are melded in the samba, as in a crucible. The *samba* is the *apoplexy* of the court, it is the pyrrhic victory of the bedroom. In it, the heavy sovereign conquers the light *mameluca* [a woman of mixed African and indigenous race]. In it are absorbed the hatreds of color. The *samba* is—if you will permit me the expression—a kind of pot, into which enter, separately, dark coffee and pale milk, and out of which is poured, homogeneous and harmonic, the hybrid *café-com-leite*: coffee with milk.[20]

The *índia* of the story is here replaced by the *mameluca*, the *zamba* with *café-com-leite*. The proliferation in Brazil of terms for highly specified kinds of racial mixing is truly mind-boggling. Dozens of designations are in popular use.[21] It is of no surprise that in the fictional constructions it is the woman who is figured as source or product of miscegenation. For obvious historical reasons, it is more accurate to suggest that it was the mameluca who absorbed Portuguese, *male* whiteness, even if it is figured as milk. In fact, early European writings frequently figured the conquest of Brazil as a maternal process: Europe giving suck to the "savages," offering up sweet Christian Humanism—the milk of human kindness. Of course colonization is never that gentle. And the milk proffered by the Portuguese to both African and indigenous women was another bodily fluid altogether. It is doubtful whether racial *hatred* was absorbed in quite the "homogeneous and harmonic" way described here. The erotic undertones of this story, however, point to the way in which racial difference has been romanticized in Brazil. It is particularly the woman of mixed race who figurally absorbs the fear of racial resistance in her sexual conquerability.

This mameluca, like the cabocla of the earlier story, is of course fictional. And yet there has been a fascinating appropriation of the "Indian" as a figure within black cultural expressions in Brazil. This is not to say that there has not been literal indigenous influence on black music and dance forms. In fact, it is difficult to separate this from the figurative influence. Siqueira's thesis is of interest because he attempts to ground the figurative cabocla in a literal historical account—based on etymology—which would reaffirm an indigenous cultural presence in popular forms. Certainly samba as it is danced in interior regions of the northeast of Brazil, where many people are of indigenous descent, resembles closely the descriptions we have of seventeenth-century indigenous dances. The posture is more stooped toward the ground, and the feet shuffle in a minute pattern, more earthbound than the springy coastal forms.

Most Brazilian folklorists derive the word *samba* not from the Cariri but from an African source. The Ki-Kongo word *semba* is translated in Portuguese as *umbigada*, meaning "a blow struck with the belly button." In the earliest documented forms of the dance in Brazil, this gesture was used by the dancer in the center of a circle of spectators to call the next dancer to take a turn. Edison Carneiro argues that it is this gesture which unifies almost all variations on the samba in Brazil.[22] The same gesture was also recorded by the Portuguese among Angolans in Africa during the period of slavery. The dominant school of Brazilian ethnologists has been, historically, profoundly Africanist and has tended to obscure indigenous influences on the culture. Hence, in the literature on samba, Siqueira's thesis sticks out like a sore thumb.

Based on similarities to rhythms and dances recorded in Angola, it is probably fair to say that samba is essentially a Kongo rhythm and expression. But it has certainly absorbed other cultural influences. It has also absorbed the eroticization of miscegenation. And while samba is even popularly regarded as essentially African, the women who dance it professionally—in the carnaval or in tourist shows—are all called *mulatas*, regardless of their color. I myself am white and blue-eyed, and I have danced with shining jet black women, but in the context of our dancing samba we were all mulatas. When I have danced particularly well, I have always been told that this is evidence of some black blood. This is not a literal misapprehension of my race. It is a statement of belief that the meaningfulness of race is culture and that a commitment to culture can result in an accrual of racial spiritual energy. *Mulatto* is a term which has in this country recently become regarded as not merely a racial but also a racist designation. Opposition to the word is based on its etymology: from Spanish *mulato*, *mulo*, from Latin *mulus*, mule. The mule is a freak of nature, a mismatched hybrid, useful for labor but unable to sustain itself as a line. The mule is incapable of reproducing. The mulata of the samba is eroticized, of course—but does she really embody the ideals of racial miscegenation in Brazil? Or is she perceived as that which does not produce or reproduce its own color, but absorbs the European pallor in a sensuality which allows for not only progressive whitening but also a dissolution of the potential for racial anger? This may be the underlying perception or desire in white depictions of samba. But popular samba perceives—and constantly reaffirms and *reproduces*—its color.

It seems perfectly obvious that these ways of talking about race are highly figurative and that the stories told about samba's racial history are fairy tales. But none of this is very far from the typical discussions of the significance of race in Brazil. Miscegenation is central to Brazilians' self-conception. To begin to understand this, an American from the United States must first get beyond her own cultural presuppositions of racial categories. As the historian Carl Degler has bluntly put it, "In Brazil the mulatto is not a Negro, whereas in the United States he is."[23] That is, in part, why miscegenation has been perceived as a process of "whitening" in Brazil, and not here. This is the fundamental difference in the two countries' understanding of race. Brazil has, as Degler again succinctly terms it, the "mulatto escape hatch":

when a society develops a place for the mulatto as occurred in Brazil, then certain other responses to the presence of black men in a white-dominated society, such as those that were worked out in the United States, for example, are foreclosed.[24]

But there is more. The person of mixed race stands not only as evidence of relations between blacks and whites but as what Degler rightly calls a "condensation" of those relations. In other words, he becomes the central character, supercharged with significance, in the story that Brazilians tell each other about their history.

Again, Gilberto Freyre's account—although clearly anachronistic to contemporary social scientists—holds considerable sway with the general population. Freyre's most influential work, translated as *The Masters and the Slaves: A Study in the Development of Brazilian Civilization*, is in large part devoted to descriptions of the sexual relations between blacks and whites. Race and sexuality are not just inextricably intertwined; they practically become interchangeable terms. Freyre details the circumstances of interracial sexual contact and its consequences (not merely mixed-blood progeny but also epidemic sexually transmitted diseases and uncontrolled promiscuity). Freyre writes:

> It is generally said that the Negro corrupted the sexual life of Brazilian society by precociously initiating the sons of the family into physical love. But it was not the Negro woman who was responsible for this; it was the woman slave.[25]

Of course, what he means is that the social *structure* of slavery was responsible for a corrupted system of sexual exchange. But the weird locution, which, irony erased, would assign sexual blame to a woman first for her race and second for her enslavement, is actually part of the subtle narrative that still circulates. For all of Freyre's gestures toward Boas's antiracist social theories, his account of "Brazilian civilization" has strange resonances with popular racial-erotic images. The typical narrative reverses the roles of sexual power. If the black woman's bondage forced her to be sexually submissive and her bondage itself was eroticized, she gets inscribed rather as the sexual "initiator," binding boys in "physical love." This version of the story allows for a mixed-race child to be born not of rape and repression but of black exuberance and white naiveté. While blacks in the United States perceive their own racial mixing as the product of rape, Brazilians rarely and uneasily concede to a history of sexual violence.

Since the 1970s, however, some mixed-race Brazilians have begun to identify as black. Both academics and political activists promoting such affiliation have been derided by some as blindly adopting U.S. social standards. And it is true that the slow and tentative "browning" of Brazil over the last two decades has had the mark of U.S. cultural influence.[26] In fact, the English word *brown* is black chic, and its reference is not just to skin tone but also to the hardest-working man in show business.[27] But who would argue that the importation of Black Power aesthetics in Brazil has anything to do with cultural imperialism? "Browning" is self-conscious political affiliation with U.S. blacks. It is a reappropriation of the mixed-race figure which was eroticized, feminized, and thus effectively depoliticized as the mulata sambista.

But it's not by any means only through foreign aesthetic influences that Brazilians manage to complicate the racial politics of their music and dance. Even the deepest, most rooted African traditions in Brazil have an intricate language for speaking of race. Traditional African religions as they are practiced in Brazil go by a number of names. In Bahia, where the communities of worship of West African gods are most pervasive, the religion is known as candomblé. Candomblé's beliefs and practices are derived from those of the Yoruba people of southwestern Nigeria. It is an ancient, complex, and powerfully beautiful belief system in which spirituality is expressed through sophisticated rhythmic structures and divinity makes itself present in the bodies of dancers. This is what is commonly referred to as "possessional" dance, but I am disinclined to use the term because of its connotations of violence or violation. The dancer in the candomblé studies for an extended period in order to be able to open her body to the divinity which will serve and be served by her community.

The houses of candomblé which appear to have remained closest to Yoruba tradition are said to be of the *kêto* or *nagô* "nation." The word *nation* was used during the period of the slave trade to identify not the land of origin of Africans arriving in Brazil but rather the port out of which they had been shipped. The "nations" were in effect trade names. But the Africans in Brazil reclaimed the terms as a way of identifying cultural affinities. Blacks in Brazil today can often specify the nation of their great-grandparents. Differences in candomblé practice are marked by nation, although the members of the houses may be descended from other areas of Africa. While relatively small in number, the kêto and nagô houses are highly regarded in the religious community at large and have certainly been favored by the Africanist ethnographic community of which I have written. Far more common, however, are houses of the angola nation, or of the "candomblé de caboclo." The pantheon of these houses is still based on that of the Yoruba gods, or orixás. But in these houses the figure of the "Indian" has been imbued with both spiritual and political significance. Here, the caboclo enters the canon as a figure mediating between the divine and the temporal. The caboclo spirit is, in the words of the folklorist Raúl Lody, "the free hunter, true prototype of him who would not allow himself to be enslaved."[28] In other words, the caboclo is an idealized image of the resistant black.

In the South of the United States, it is sometimes perceived that while some actual racial mixing took place between African and native Americans, this has been exaggerated in black folklore and popular culture. Zora Neale Hurston wrote, with tongue firmly in cheek, that she was the only southern black not matrilineally descended from an Indian chief.[29] Hurston's comment suggests that an African American claim of "Indianness" is based on a desire to assume a lighter color. But racial identification with indigenous peoples might be read as a much stronger political affiliation—one which comprehends not only color but a history of cultural and political repression as well. In Brazil, a person's caboclo or Indian aspect is a quality which may come not from blood inheritance but from commitment to the ideal of freedom. My own Indian protector spirits have been identified at moments of my most energetic and muscular dancing or at times (often the same ones) when I evidenced a furious protectiveness of my own sexual independence.

Michael Taussig[30] has demonstrated that the figure of the Indian has always served as a means for the colonist to justify his project: he is the human embodiment of wildness, of a nature which must be controlled. In Brazil, this figure has been retained for deployment in various political contexts. The indigenous population was ceremoniously consecrated in the same recent constitution which prohibited racism (to the same non-effect: prospectors' regular slaughter of Amazonian people continues to go virtually unpunished). Interestingly, the Indian was invoked at the time of Brazil's independence as the image of a land rejecting Portugal's attempts at control. This doesn't mean that the formation of the republic boded well for real indigenous Brazilians. But the caboclo as a sign of an ideal, unhierarchical Brazilian society is associated with nationalistic images—including the national flag and colors.[31] Worshiping the caboclo allows black Brazilians to express their Brazilian nationalism while rejecting the existing social stratifications within their nation.

The dances of the candomblé, as I said, come from a Yoruba tradition—even those dances designated of the Angola nation. Samba appears to have been derived from Kongo-Angolan moves. And yet there are certain similarities, the most striking being the circle formation of participants in the dances. In the candomblé, the circle of dancers moves counterclockwise until one or several receive a divine spirit. At this moment, the entity, held no longer to be a mere dancer but an incorporation of divine energy, moves to the center of the circle, which is called a *roda*, or wheel. Each god presents a particular choreography, obliquely mimetic of a divine principle. Yemanjá, goddess of the sea, undulates, her shoulders tremulous as the sea's surface.

In the *samba de roda*, the most traditional form of the dance as it is danced in Bahia, the circle does not rotate, but the participants stand, clap, and take turns going to the center. This is a separate tradition from the roda of the candomblé. It is only in the candomblé de caboclo that samba is considered an integral part of the candomblé ceremony. When the caboclo spirit comes down, he sambas. The roda is fixed. Ethnographers have been uncomfortable in classifying the *samba de caboclo* with other candomblé dances. This may be because of the purist, Africanist tendencies in the Brazilian ethnographic community. But even within the religious community, the very use of the term *samba* to designate the caboclo spirit's dance seems to be a way of blurring the distinction between the divine and the profane. Defenders of the candomblé de caboclo have argued that the term *samba de caboclo* is a reductive or even derogatory classification. The caboclo, however, is precisely intent on breaking down barriers, releasing strictures such as those between the sacred and the secular.

In the candomblés which do not entertain the caboclo, samba can also occur, but only after a ceremony has ended. The secular drumming and dancing are an afterthought, and they may be encouraged as a way of redeeming an evening in which the divine turnout has been disappointing. The songs of the candomblé ceremonies are sung in Yoruba, but the samba, including samba de caboclo, is almost always sung in Portuguese. Samba within the candomblé community is marked by what is called *sotaque*, or accent, as in a foreign or regional accent. What this means is that the lyrics to the songs pun on certain terms used in the candomblé. Bawdy jokes are made, which are only intelligible to those initiated into the community. The puns play on Yoruba. The ethnographer Maria Teixeira recorded one such song, a samba which plays on the word *efó*, a dish of cooked greens with palm oil served during many candomblé rituals—and a favorite of the caboclo.

Eu fui comer um efó	I went to eat efó
Na casa de Pai Dendê	In the house of Father Dendê
O efó saiu mal feito	The efó was badly made
Eu quero efó, dê no que der	I want efó, come what may
	(*I want to fuck what I can*)
Mamãe quando fô dê	Mama, when you go, give
	(*Mama, when you fuck*)
Lembranças a quem fô de lá[32]	My regards to those you meet
	(*My regards to those who fuck*)

Recombining the Yoruba and Portuguese syllables turns *efó* into *foder*: to fuck. This kind of mixing of the sacred and profane may seem surprising. But the puns can only be *merely* profane to those who are outside of candomblé's body of knowledge. So even though the samba is an entrance of the profane into a sacred space, it serves to reaffirm the cohesion of the "povo de santo": the people of the saints, or orixás.

SAMBA

Samba in this context can also pun visually on the candomblé dances. While the dance is considered secular, it may encode references to divine choreographies. In this way, the *roda de samba* serves a complementary purpose to that of the *roda de santo*, or the circle formation of the candomblé. The roda here is an inclusionary (or exclusionary) boundary, so that while there is a seeming boundary between the candomblé and the samba, the latter form reinforces the boundary of the African religious community. Teixeira argues that this does not debase the notion of a divine circle but rather raises the human body and its motion to a sacred ground. The roda de samba is the space in which the individual body and *its* intelligence mediate between spheres.

> The center of the Roda de Santo, through *axé*, relives the mythic drama of the Orixás; it is the divinities that assume the stage with all their refinement, potency and decorum. In the Roda de Samba, it is the cult of the body which assumes relevance.[33]

Axé is Yoruba for pure potentiality, divine energy, or, in the translation of Robert Farris Thompson which has always struck me as the most accurate, the power-to-make-things-happen. When Teixeira says that axé allows divine entities to take the stage—and the bodies of the dancers—of the candomblé, she means that it is the presence of the orixás that brings significance to the dance. But in the roda de samba, the *human body* assumes a heightened level of significance.

Axé is not restricted to the context of the candomblé. The power-to-make-things-happen can exist within a secular rhythm. It is not any samba which provokes motion in the irresistible way I described above. A certain degree of potentiality is required. When one is dancing, the parts of the body respond to the various instruments and patterns being played. And the parts of the body respond when a given musician begins to play with particular axé—which is not by any means to be confused with volume.

I spoke of the roda as an inclusive or exclusive boundary, and nowhere in Brazilian dance is this more powerfully represented than in the *roda de capoeira*. Capoeira is another Kongo-derived tradition, a fighting game performed to percussive music. The moves are fluid, elegant, and potentially devastating if used for effect. Blacks in Brazil trained capoeira for defense of the *quilombos*—communities composed of escaped slaves—and its practice was prohibited by white authorities. But the roda was a protective circle for the training capoeiristas. The changing rhythm of the musicians served as a warning to fighters, and if an overseer approached, the moves were modified to appear to be "merely" a samba. Even within the game of capoeira, dance serves as a disguise. The two players at the center of the roda sway back and forth rhythmically in a step called the *ginga*, and it is only out of this seemingly imbalanced and unprotected attitude that capoeira's kicks and sweeps can be deployed.

As Muniz Sodré has observed,[34] one of the oldest and most popular capoeira songs is an ironic twisting of the sentiments of whites in Brazil during the slavery period. The song simply repeats the phrase *cala a boca, moleque*—"shut your mouth, black boy." The words are provocative, and if I say they echo the old white attitudes, I might also suggest they articulate a contemporary sentiment—in a slightly more complicated sense. I say complicated, because the overt sentiment expressed by white Brazilian society today is not only tolerance of but affection for the musicality of black culture. But the unstated message given by whites is still "cala a boca moleque—e vá sambar." Shut up and dance. The provocation of the capoeira song, though, is a directive much more dangerous: if you can't speak the truth with your mouth, speak it with your feet— not in a patter of meaningless, endlessly expendable energy but in a precisely aimed *benção*, or blessing, a kick which plants the sole of the foot on the chest of one's opponent. A blessing is a benediction, good talk, the appropriate response. Frantz Fanon wrote that this is the language of the politicization of the oppressed: "He of whom *they* have never stopped saying that the only language he understands is that of force, decides to give *utterance by force*."[35] Capoeira has always been a language of black resistance.

Both the candomblé and capoeira were aggressively suppressed by white authorities until the participation of middle-class whites became impossible to ignore. The tourist industry also saw the potential exotic appeal. Now there is even official sanctioning and financial support—under particular and controlled circumstances. But even during the period of prohibition, both candomblé dance and capoeira were sustained in the roda de samba, through gestural and rhythmic reference: *sotaque*. In the layered rhythms of samba, the strong accent which is suspended is the silencing of other forms.

That gap is filled by direct incorporation of candomblé and capoeira moves. The percussionists may even make reference to the rhythms and songs of these forms. In the midst of a samba, the *agôgô* bell may begin to play the clave of the orixá Xangô's rhythm or the *atabaque* drummer may start to slap out a capoeira beat. But more likely the reference will be subtle. In the body of the dancer, it may be multiple. The feet shift rapidly in the pattern of the dance of the caboclo-identified bush divinity, Oxossi. The hips flash the fire of the storm goddess Iansã, and the shoulders shimmer like the surface of Yemanjá's waters. The whole of the dance is seemingly set off balance in the deceptive sway of capoeira's ginga, but it hides a potential blow. Or the blow can actualize itself: mid-samba one can sweep the feet out from under one's partner in a move taken straight from capoeira. This is known as *samba duro*: hard samba.

How does one narrate the interrelation of the dances? Once could construct another story, set perhaps on a sugarcane plantation in Bahia, where, hidden, the Yoruba formed their circles of divinity and the Kongo formed their circles of political anger. And the circles became one circle and the rhythms overlapped, and the sacred slapped its belly against the profane and samba was born. But it didn't happen like that. African and indigenous communities were dispersed. Their histories were ruptured. Their own narrative structures were shattered. The culture which grows out of vio-

SAMBA

lence maintains its echoes of historical and rhythmic disjunction. The rodas of candomblé, capoeira, and samba can't be straightened out into a linear account. Samba is as much a fragmentation of a holy black body as it is a healing of spiritual and political wounds.

But the rhythm is gorgeous. The body is gorgeous. It tells the story I can't tell here—one which is aesthetic, spiritual, and political. What happened next? The dancing body itself was dispersed. Some dancers stayed in Bahia, and they still dance in a roda, swathed in the huge white skirts of the candomblé ceremonies. Some went to Rio, where they institutionalized the *escolas de samba*, carnaval samba schools where today white TV soap opera stars parade topless on floats, meagerly twitching their bottoms in a weak imitation of the real thing. Some refused to ride, or would have, had they been invited: they remained on the asphalt, scraping ever-new inventiveness out of their silver shoes. It is as impossible to say which is more "authentic"—samba in Rio or Bahia—as it is to make sense of a simple historical account of how it got there. The Rio sambista in silver shoes, in all likelihood black despite her "mulata" classification, may dance consumed with axé.

I believe I came to understand the significance of the body in time only when I learned to samba. Of course as a white American from the United States I have been suspect, and it was perhaps partly my tenacity in the face of this suspicion that made me understand resistance in the dance. I have been challenged. Once it happened in a house of candomblé in Bahia. The caboclo arrived and spun about furiously, then stopped abruptly and pointed at my feet. I was pushed into the roda, and I danced as if to save my life. I was fully aware that the caboclo was not so much interested in the speed of my feet as in my commitment to saying something meaningful with them. The exigency of the caboclo is the weight I feel in my bones and muscles each time I attempt to write, in words, about the significance of resistant culture.

Once the challenge happened on a little *praça*, or plaza, off the beach in the Flamengo section of Rio. Some members of the famous Mangueira samba school were jamming and swilling beer. A seasoned mulata, fiftyish, short, stocky, and tanked to the gills, was decked out in the school colors: hot pink visor and T-shirt, lime-green eye shadow, hot pants and plastic shoes. She eyed me over and put me to work: I did a respectable little solo, ending with a subdued swivel and then a shiver in the hips. She took her turn: a lengthy, hilarious trip-step in no rush at all, ending with pure glory. She glanced at me, licked her fingertips, and held them, wet, millimeters from the V of her hot pants as she took a deep, luxuriating grind down to the ground. She busted my chops.

For all of the anxiety which samba's eroticism causes many from the United States, whether for reasons of morality or politics, I have found its *auto*erotic potential to be extraordinarily liberating. In a culture in which racism and sexism are articulated in each other's terms, I was beginning to get some kind of

SAMBA

bodily comprehension of the race politics of Brazil—
what was called an accrual of black blood, or Indian
protector spirits. Samba, like capoeira, does not employ
full frontal blows. Part of its strength is seduction—even
apparent vulnerability. But the female sambista must
assume her sexuality—not as the coffeepot, receptacle
of some wan, milky fluid, but as Iansã's self-sufficient
whirlwind of the hips. She takes a man if she wants one!
It would be highly idealistic—and wrong—to suggest
that this is the reality of a Brazilian underclass woman.
But it is an ideal expressed by her in the samba.

She can be funny, terrifying, painfully beautiful—
but above all she must be eloquent. She is committed
to saying something that has not been and cannot be
spoken. Wherever she is, whatever color she is, her
feet have to speak, and they have to speak not only of
beauty but also of her own belief and resistance.

2. Divine Choreography and the Embodiment of Metaphor

Choreography means the writing of dance. The notion itself seems self-contradictory. Motion is, necessarily, ephemeral. Writing sticks. While we may suggest that dance is "readable," how does the body's motion get inscribed? Earlier I said that Western musical notation is not adequate to the polymeters of Brazilian music. But dance notation has long been recognized as inadequate even to Western forms. Probably the most durable and influential of modern choreographic writing systems is labanotation, named after its inventor, Rudolph Laban.[1] Innovative contemporary choreographers have made use of computer imaging. But if notions such as rhythm-bending and axé cannot be programmed into a drum machine, divine motion can hardly be accommodated for by these inscriptive methods. African religious dance in the New World is perhaps the cultural phenomenon which most markedly demonstrates our inability to textualize or represent that culture. In *Mumbo Jumbo*, Ishmael Reed writes of an "epidemic" called Jes Grew which appears to be the pan-African cultural tradition:

> Jes Grew was an influence which sought its text, and whenever it thought it knew the location of its words and Labanotations it headed in that direction. . . . If it could not find its Text then it would be mistaken for entertainment. Its basic dances were said to have been recorded by the secretary to the first Seedy Fellow himself.[2]

Reed tells us Jes Grew's text gets destroyed. And the notation of divine pan-African dance may always be thwarted. I write of it here because of a divine invocation, understanding that the project may self-destruct.

I didn't just choose this project. Ifá ordained it, and my mother translated the command offhandedly but with an incontestable authority. (It was so like her blithely to demand the impossible. She regularly asked for French perfumes extravagantly beyond one's means.) My *mãe de santo*, mother of saints, the priestess who baptized me into the candomblé, felt that writing was an acceptable activity for me, but only secondary to, and preferably in the service of, dance. I'm sure she found me a curiosity: a gringa determined to embody the saints' grace. I was introduced to her as a dancer, and she immediately put me to the test. In her receiving room, she made one of her daughters of saint put on a scratchy old recording of candomblé drums and asked for the orixás one by one. She called in the daughters from the compound to watch, laugh and correct me. Supreme humiliation! And yet I was a little proud of what I knew—these gestures I'd learned by hook or by crook through classes in New York and at the university in Bahia, through carnaval groups, friends, and just watching mesmerized at public ceremonies. I knew (after a fashion) almost every orixá's dance. Step by step, I was winning her over, as she slapped her thighs in amusement. For the most part, she compared me favorably to her patient and good-humored daughters, whom she took this occasion to lambaste as overweight, lethargic, or just plain ugly. Even if my training had been unorthodox, she appreciated my evident resolve. A few New York downtown dance studios may fill up with earnest (if a little ridiculous) women like myself yearning to mimic correctly an African god's motion, but in Brazil it's quite unusual to learn candomblé dance outside of the initiation process. She considered herself a studious woman as well—and a *trained* dancer. And so of course, despite her general approbation, she would occasionally interrupt my performance with cutting disdain: "Who taught you Ogun's arms like that? *Que merda*, those who don't know go like that, but we who understand these things do *this*." When she moved, an almost obscene grace filled the room; she was portentous with axé. Mother Aildes retaught me everything I thought I knew about dance. It was under her tutelage that it became meaningful. Her body was full of complaints, and it wasn't long before it stopped being useful to her as a vessel in this inadequate, brutal little world. Now her breath resides in a jar and her body underground in a plot about an hour outside Rio. Her breath comes back like a wind, smoky, hot, maternal, loving and disdainful, raunchy, cosmopolitan—she was a diva!—and she reminds me of what she divined: my orixás, and how to feed them: write about these dances!

The dances of the candomblé constitute a part of its liturgy. But there are other forms of more literal inscription in the religion. Before I begin to address the specific issue of candomblé choreography, or written motion, I want to examine some of the other forms of divine inscription in the Afro-Brazilian tradition. What I hope to demonstrate is that this tradition defines writing in a way which could recomplicate Western assumptions about the fixity of inscription and its relationship to the body, motion, and sexuality.

Narrowly speaking, the notion of a liturgical body of writing is called Ifá by the Yoruba and their sisters and brothers in Brazil. Ifá is the name of an orixá, but it is also used to refer to the divination system over which he rules. Ifá divination in Nigeria is traditionally performed with sixteen palm nuts, or with a chain that carries eight seed-halves from a fruit called opélé. The results of a series of hand-to-hand manipulations of the nuts, if the seed chain is not read directly, are recorded by the diviner in a tray containing a fine wood dust. The mathematics of Ifá tells us that there are 256 possible configurations of marks in the dust of the divining tray. The Yoruba say that the priest must memorize several sacred poems for each configuration, one of which will be the divine response to the questions of the community.[3]

In Brazil, Ifá divination usually takes place through the casting of cowrie shells. The system has been simplified. Some diviners continue to trace their patterns on a tray, but more often divine responses are read directly off the pattern of the cast shells. This was the procedure of my own mother. Ifá reading is considered the only reliable script of divine will, although in less important cases (depending on the orthodoxy of the reader) it may be replaced by a reading of standard playing cards, or even the Tarot.

The dust of the divining tray appears to have been somewhat effaced by the passage of violent time. But divine writing, however seemingly ephemeral, persists, and in the more syncretic areas—notably Rio de Janeiro—designs are fingered into the sand of the beaches.[4] The patterns incorporate images from the Yoruba, Kongo, and Catholic traditions. They are called *pontos riscados*, or marked or scratched points. *Riscar* means both to mark and to scratch out, or delete. The pontos riscados are points in the sense of a focusing of energy, but also in that they point the way for a particular divinity to come down. They are of course very similar in this sense to the better-known *vévés*, or cornmeal ground-drawings of the vodun religion in

SAMBA

Haiti. These patterns are not meant to textualize or describe the various divinities but rather to *call them down*. They are not, that is, evocative images so much as invocative. This may have something to do with their ephemeral character: a god cannot be pinned down to one spot. The Haitians trample their vévés when the gods come down to dance. Dance negates writing.

The Brazilian pontos riscados are also sometimes drawn on the ground with chalk, a quick-erasing medium. One familiar ponto has achieved a certain degree of fixity, having become the logo for the notoriously tough capoeira school of the late great master Bimba.

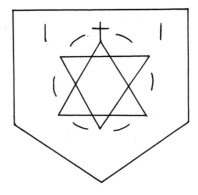

The logo is impressed on the school's uniform T-shirts, and a few of the most committed students have tattooed it onto their skin, unerasable.

This bodily inscription is not so much a spin-off of traditional African notions of writing as it is a return to the site of divine representation. In Yorubaland, scarification, or writing *on* the body, signifies one's specific ethnic, political, and religious affiliations. It is beautification achieved through pain. The beauty perceived by the Yoruba in these scars cannot be separated from their significance of affiliation. Westerners' aversion to the appearance of the scars may be articulated as not ethnocentric but humane: the scars trace the violence and the pain of their inscription. But for the Yoruba they mark a double, keloid healing: they mark the place where the wounds of an individual have healed, but they also mark the place where her individualism was mutilated in order to heal her into her society. This doesn't negate the violence.[5] All socialization might be seen as a violence against individuals, and individualism. The Yoruba literalize this in a scar. We find it somewhat more difficult to see our own.

Scarification and the implements used to perform it fall under the domain of the orisa Ogun, the god of metalworking and war.[6] In the New World, this cultural practice was largely repressed, although small incisions are still made—notably on the head and upper arm—in candomblé ritual.[7] But decorative scarification in Brazil was replaced with another kind of bodily demarcation during the slavery period. Captive Africans were not permitted to mark their own affiliations in their skin. They received instead the physical traces of the violence of slavery in scars which were sometimes intended to mark them into servitude, as well as incidental scars of corporal punishment which are equally significant. Both metaphorical and metonymic, the scars of slavery, like the tattoos of Holocaust victims, signify a violence perpetrated against both individuals and a race.

SAMBA

The practice of ritual scarification was repressed, as were other modes of political, spiritual, and aesthetic representation. Thus far I have been describing Afro-Brazilian forms of inscription in quite a literal sense: lines traced, whether in dust, earth, or flesh. But what of the figurative aspects of writing in this tradition—or the aspects of figurative writing? What defines figuration in the system? Visual arts are the most obvious place to consider representation. The Yoruba in Nigeria today say that none of their woodcarvings or brass castings *represent* the oriṣas. But there are some ancient stonecarvings which are said to depict divinities. It is not entirely clear whether the practice of divine representation in sculpture has died out or if the attribution of divine significance occurs only in retrospect, as the physical object accrues a temporal distance from its human creation. But even in the unusual cases of oriṣa representation, the Yoruba expressly say that they do not worship the object, which contains in itself no divine properties. The oriṣas are principles of nature which precede human creative potential. They manifest themselves in the objects of nature: stones, trees, water, meteorological phenomena, animals—and the human body. Visual arts are merely a manner of recording the stories which ground the principles of divinity.

There is much debate surrounding the classification of Yoruba belief as mono- or polytheistic, because the Yoruba have always held the idea of a supreme god, the god of gods, Ọlọrun. Ọlọrun is the one divinity which could never be represented, or even made oblique reference to in matter, as he is the truth beyond our knowledge. He never comes down in the body of a dancer. He can only be communicated with through Ifá. Our relation with the other oriṣas is much more immediate and intimate. Some Yoruba speak to the question of classification of their belief by saying it is fundamentally and metaphysically monotheistic, but practically and experientially polytheistic. This confusing response should probably convince us that there was something inadequate about the question in the first place. These classifications can't accommodate the system. And of course the most insidious thing about the question is that it implicitly demands comparison with Christian (and perhaps Muslim) belief, as though these forms had priority.

Candomblé is a syncretic faith, product of a violent cultural encounter. It demands not only a comparison of Catholic and Yoruba beliefs but also their mutual approximation. When Africans in Brazil first assimilated the orixás to Catholic saints—and Ọlọrun to the Christian God—it was out of necessity and fear of retribution. But over the centuries, the approximation has solidified. Candomblé worshipers find Saint Barbara and Iansã to be two terms for the same principle.[8] And the European-pressed chromolithographs of the Catholic saints are said to be representations of the orixás. But while the saints are, for the most part, depicted as white, the orixás are recognized as being African in origin.

On the candomblé altars, one finds both Catholic chromolithographs and sculptures which are clearly from the African tradition. But the Brazilians, like the Yoruba in Nigeria, do not create images of the gods.

SAMBA

Visual arts—in sculpture or paint—which make reference to the orixás do so obliquely. They may be representations of human figures in a state of incorporating divine energy (what is frequently referred to as "possession"). These are called *oxés*. Or they may be representations of the objects and implements associated with the specific divinities. These include the iron implements of Ogun, his *ferramentas*, or ironworks. Other orixás are supplied with swords, fans, flywhisks and axes—tools of their trades. But the sword is never used by the orixá in a literal act of stabbing. It is rather placed in his hands at the moment he presents himself in the body of a dancer. He uses it to become fully himself.

These physical objects, then, don't represent the orixás. Divinity cannot be represented mimetically but only contiguously or metonymically. The manifestation of the orixás is pure presence. Human beings can't reproduce them. The Yoruba understand that the bodies of men and women are carved out, like wooden dolls, in the womb by the orişa Ọbatala. How could that process be inverted? We are not the shapers of divinity. We are rather created as works of art.

We recognize ourselves as objects of art when we dance the orixás' choreographies. The dancer in the candomblé is not considered to be an artist. Individual creativity is not admired as a characteristic of the worshiper. But the community may take pleasure in the excellence of a body as a vessel for an orixá. Physical strength and beauty may be appreciated by the community, as they will be appreciated by the orixá. But what animates the religious dance is not personal genius. And often an old or feeble body contains so much axé that its motion in the dance far exceeds what should be physically possible. When the observers of a ceremony see this kind of transformation, they recognize the body as divinely gorgeous. Maya Deren, writing of the related and similar religious dances of Haiti, noted that the gods of vodun, called the loa, are always perceived as the authors of glorious motion—and this actively negates any sense of the artistic prowess or individuality of the dancer:

> . . . if, in the crowded peristyle, one remarks, among all these bodies which move with such homogeneity, one whose movements exceed this generality, become spectacular—this is a sign that a loa arrives. For if the mark of a man's dedication to the loa is selfless anonymity, the mark of a loa's devotion to man is his most elaborated, realized manifestation. Therefore, virtuosity is the province of divinity. Only the loa are virtuosi.[9]

Deren argues that Haitian religious dance is not, in itself, a particularly demanding form, as it can be learned by anyone, and that by definition it cannot require special skill. My own experiences in Brazil have been somewhat contradictory to this. My own mother of saints and many other of my friends who dance within the candomblé regard themselves as highly trained. They speak often of *técnica*—technique—and use specific Yoruba terminology to describe different kinds of motion. Even the seemingly most involuntary of movements, the shivering of the upper torso which usually immediately precedes divine incorporation, is designated as *ejeká*, which is Yoruba for shoulders. The term refers to all isolated motion of the shoulder blades, which is a marked feature of many orixá choreographies (and, for the untrained, supremely difficult). The study of the orixá dances is the study of divine liturgy and is taken very seriously. It marks one not as an artist but as a religious scholar, and it demonstrates the seriousness of belief.

"Who taught you Ogun's arms like that? *Que merda*, those who don't know go like that, but we who understand these things do *this*." My mother of saints scolded me for excessive mimesis. The orixá choreographies are danced in two senses within the candomblé ceremonies. They are danced, as I have said, in the body which incorporates divine energy. This is the case after the orixá has come down and made him- or herself present at the celebration. The coming down is marked by an evident change in the motion of the body. Divine animation is absolutely recognizable to the members of the community. When it occurs, the body of the dancer is taken into a back room where it is clothed in the preferred raiments of the god. The implements are also taken up—in the case of Ogun, the great sword of his violent potential. When Ogun emerges, triumphant, it is he who dances in the center of the circle of worship, and he evidences his glory.[10]

The other sense in which the choreographies are performed is as an invocation to the orixás, prior to their descent. This was the kind of dance which I was replicating in my mother of saints' receiving room. In the candomblé, invocative dance is generally subdued, but it is not haphazard. Its subtlety is meaningful. Before Ogun comes down and takes his sword, the dancers in the candomblé perform his choreography empty-handed. The emptiness is a request for fulfillment—not by the granting of the sword, which is incidental, but by the presence of the god. It is a request for the granting of meaningfulness. Calling this dance invocative recalls the pontos riscados, which I said were invocative inscription. The pontos riscados are not meant to be read as descriptions of the orixás. Neither are these invocative dances to be read—or performed—as evocations or representations of divinity. They don't yet carry this meaning.

When I was first taught Ogun's dance, outside of the candomblé, I was told that he carried a heavy blade, which he brandished threateningly in his right hand, striking his right arm repeatedly against the left. As he struck his powerful forearms together, he pitched himself forward in a zigzag of broad, fearsome strides: three to the right, three to the left. Of course, there was no heavy blade, and there is no heavy blade taken up until Ogun himself takes over the dance. Truth be told, the physical blade Ogun receives in a genuine ceremony is not heavy, not iron, but most often light laminated chrome. But it is understood as indicative of iron and of weight. The friends who taught me Ogun's choreography—ostensibly his invocative dance—were active in the carnaval groups in Bahia known as *afoxés*. The afoxés take the candomblé rhythms and dances into the street at carnaval, in a celebration of their aesthetic and political strength. When they taught me Ogun's choreography, they seemed to turn their own arms into iron blades. Their palms flattened out to a sharp edge, and sparks seemed to fly at the point of their connection. The dance told a story: it represented Ogun as an embodiment of iron and political potential.

My mother of saints had seen this happen before, and her offense was evident. The invocative dance cannot be mimetic. "We who understand these things do *this*." She performed the same choreography, but the movement had become completely abstracted. Whereas my brutally referential thwacking of arm against arm would have been recognizable as a striking of blades, her gesture was a fluid vague crossing and uncrossing that might have been read as suggestive of anything from water to wheat. It is not meant to be read. It is not meant to suggest. We are the suggestion of divinity.

Mother Aildes was an intellectual, a scholar of the candomblé who watched bemused as its forms became increasingly literal-minded. There may be several ways of explaining this change. The explanations I give here are interesting as plausible stories, but I don't genuinely believe that any of them offers a true history of the development of a dance style. As I wrote earlier in describing the development of the samba parallel to religious and martial traditions, a linear narration in dance ethnography is never convincing historiography. There is no individual artistic will which creates or modifies a dance form. Maya Deren writes of the "collective [of vodun worshipers] as creative artist."[11] The vodun community, she says, "functions at a level superior to the

creative capacities of the individuals that make it up."
Community is one way of explaining the extraordinary
creative and modifying forces of syncretic culture,
which is always a culture under pressure to cohere.
Within candomblé belief, this could only be articulated
as the creative power of the gods themselves. To say
that the orixás themselves exert a transformative power
on culture is perhaps the only adequate narration of the
change.

But a more earthbound explanation of the aug-
mentation of the mimetic quality of orixá choreography
might point to mundaner influences. Anthropologists
have associated increased mimesis in dance with de-
creased knowledge of the oral narratives surrounding
the orixás. Margaret Thompson Drewal writes:

> In the Bahian context, where the oral liturgy is only
> vaguely understood by its users, dance can define and
> characterize the deity in a more precise way than the
> oral texts. Thus in addition to stressing *how* Ogun
> operates, that is, his dynamic qualities, the dances in
> Bahia become more literal by miming precisely *what*
> Ogun does.[12]

We might read the stylistic development as a fundamental change in the notion of divine representation
within candomblé belief. It could be regarded as a
syncretic development—an absorption of the Catholic
chromolithographs into the concept of how we perceive divinity. Perhaps after a century or so of the co-
existence of plaster saints, *oxés,* and metal implements,
the metaphoric began to rub off on the metonymic.

Or we might see this as a phenomenon which has
become exacerbated much more recently, in response

to greater liberties of religious practice over the last two decades. Worship of the orixás was prohibited for most of Brazilian history.[13] It was only when the participation of middle-class whites was perfectly apparent that authorities lifted the old codes. During the 1980s, the afoxés and other Afrocentric carnaval groups in Bahia called *blocos afro* began to harness black cultural tradition to create political change. Afro-Brazilians seeking a political coherence in the Yoruba faith may translate this need for meaning into the dance forms, as they become even more overtly, more explicitly readable.

We do read dance, which is why I have consistently referred to orixá choreography, although the dances are not choreographed in a Western sense. They still constitute a form of writing—writing through motion—which is read as meaningful in the community. The dancer in a state of an orixá's incorporation is not a writer of that dance but rather becomes the text, written by the orixá. These historical hypotheses of a shift in style do not please me, although the latter rings particularly true in my experience. But if this is a collective appeal for meaning from orixá culture, the change in form would have to be regarded as an act of divine revision, or rewriting, according to changes in the sociohistorical context. Meaning—readability—depends upon the authority of the gods.

Allowing for the power of external forces to shape our significance—giving up the illusion of radical self-determination—is perhaps most difficult for Americans in the United States who are schooled from early childhood in the virtue of Emersonian self-reliance. I want to reiterate that participation in candomblé dance is not passive submission to a violent force of "possession" but involves study and commitment to an ethos. Still, incorporating orixá energy does require an acknowledgment that we don't fully determine our own significance in the world. When one's orixás are read through Ifá, one is generally told which *dono* or *dona da cabeça* (master or mistress of the head), as well as which secondary and tertiary orixás (the *juntó* and *adjuntó*), influence one's life trajectory. The discovery of the identity of one's orixás can be profoundly disorienting if their character doesn't correspond to one's self-perception. A particularly important part of reconfiguring identity lies in the fact that the gender of the ruler of one's head does not necessarily correspond to one's own gender. In fact, more often than not a person's primary and secondary orixás are a combination of a male and a female principle.

The initiation process prepares one to incorporate all of one's orixás. But not everyone is equipped to receive divine energy. It is not the case in Yorubaland, or even in many parts of Brazil; but in Bahia, the center of candomblé activity, it is widely accepted that women are significantly more receptive to the orixás than men. The exception to this rule is the homosexual man. Actually, this is a misstatement. The very term *homosexual* is one which needs to be opened up to reconfiguration in the context of the candomblé. For that matter, so are the very terms *woman* and *man*.

The important issue of sex and sexuality in the candomblé is certainly underplayed in the ethnographic literature, but it is by no means news. Ruth Landes published her scientific study "A Cult Matriarchate and Male Homosexuality" in the *Journal of Abnormal and Social Psychology* in 1940 and followed it in 1947 with a more popular account in *City of Women*, in which she quotes Edison Carneiro, who first introduced her to a ceremony:

> "[N]o upright man will allow himself to be ridden by a god, unless he does not care about losing his manhood. . . . Some men do let themselves be ridden, and they become priests with the women; but they are known to be homosexuals."[14]

Carneiro himself was somewhat more circumspect about homosexuality in his own writings on the candomblé, but both the ethnographic community and popular knowledge have long held this to be a truism. In fact, the sexuality of men who incorporate divinity is further specified. In her scientific paper, Landes noted in greater detail that most male cult leaders and followers in Bahia were "*passive* homosexuals of note, and were vagrants and casuals of the streets."[15] Roger Bastide, similarly, noted in 1961 the common occurrence of "passive pederasty" among initiates.[16]

The understanding of homosexuality as a category of persons in Brazilian popular culture is highly complicated. In fact, in some circles, it isn't a category as such. The anthropologists Peter Fry and, more recently, Richard Parker have attempted to translate and historicize Brazilian conceptions of sexuality.[17] As Fry has shown, the traditional folk model of sexuality is based on types and positions of sexual activity. There are not "heterosexuals" and "homosexuals" but rather those

who, in popular parlance, "eat" and those who "give"—
the former signifying taking the penetrative position in
sex, the latter the penetrated. Obviously the figure
marks the distinction that Landes and Bastide called
active and passive. This opposition was the primary one
used to configure sexuality until the beginning of this
century, when medical models began to focus on
sexual object choice: enter the categories of hetero-, bi-
and homosexuality. In the late '60s, with the increased
coalescence and politicization of a gay community, a
third categorization emerged stressing acknowledgment of one's sexual orientation, and the validity of gay
sexual expressions, be they "active" or "passive." This
third phase corresponds largely to popular U.S. and
European notions of sexuality: a man who chooses to
make love to men is gay.

That strikes most Americans in the United States as
obvious. But it is a position which, while gaining currency in Brazil, is by no means taken for granted there.
Educated Brazilians (that is, those educated in *Western*
social beliefs) distinguish between straights and gays.
But those whose social education takes place outside of
Western institutions still hold firmly to the active/pas-
sive, eat/give model—and, in fact, that model is still
operative in the upper classes, even as they must nego-
tiate it with another system.

Women's sexuality in the candomblé is much less
discussed—apparently because however it is mani-
fested, it isn't perceived as threatening masculine "activity." (However, it is sometimes suggested that older
women who have diminished their sexual activity are
more suited to devotion to the saints.) Lesbianism or

bisexuality among women appears not to be disruptive in the way that male penetrative sexuality is. Men who "eat" are termed *homens* (men), while those who "give" are *bichas* (properly, a small creature or parasite; the word itself has a feminine ending, and takes the feminine article).

At first glance, what appears to a Westerner to be a constellation of figures seems highly readable. Women and bichas are not only passive and penetrable in the sexual context. They are so in the spiritual context as well. While I have stated that proscriptions of sexuality are specific to candomblé practice in Bahia, Lorand Matory has demonstrated that the metaphor of male sexual and spiritual penetrability exists in Yorubaland as well.[18] Those who receive saint are "mounted"—*montados*—as horses are mounted by riders (remember Deren's *Divine Horsemen*) and as bichas are mounted by homens.

And yet the candomblé may provide a more complex way of thinking about sexuality. In fact, the metaphors themselves are at odds with one another. The penetrator is he who *eats*—figurally consuming, absorbing the one who *gives*. Doesn't this reverse the notion of penetration? And even if the metaphor is anthropophagic, the person who "gives" is accorded the power of materializing and separating from a part of the self, which is, presumably, the body. To allow oneself to be eaten can be seen as, itself, a penetrative act. The term *bicha* also inverts the penetration metaphor, as a parasite is one who both penetrates *and* consumes another's body.

Recently, Judith Butler turned to anthropological discourse to open up the configuration of gender and sexuality. Citing Mary Douglas, who observed that the boundaries of the body often stand for social boundaries across cultures, Butler writes:

> The construction of stable bodily contours relies upon fixed sites of corporeal permeability and impermeability. Those sexual practices in both homosexual and heterosexual contexts that open surfaces and orifices to erotic signification or close down others effectively reinscribe the boundaries of the body along new cultural lines.[19]

In fact, in Brazil, the delineation of the sexual body is by no means fixed. The permeability of this body to orixá energy may be read as a metaphor for shifting social boundaries. But another way of understanding all this is to read the reinscription of boundaries—social change—as the outward manifestation of—or itself the metaphor for—the mobility of the orixás.

I have emphasized the role of the bicha in the candomblé because it demonstrates the complexity of identity in candomblé dance. But I should mention again that "male" figures—human, divine, and in-between—have differing roles in the more syncretic angola houses. The caboclo spirit which I examined in the preceding chapter can be embodied by men or women, regardless of their sexual preferences or practices. In a quite remarkable book called *The Taste of Blood: Spirit Possession in Brazilian Candomblé,* Jim Wafer notes that angola houses entertain only male caboclo spirits. In other words, the caboclos, "at least in their materialized form, live in an exclusively masculine world. But a world in which there is only one sex is a world that is sexually undifferentiated."[20] I have already written of the caboclo as a figure of political resistance, and Wafer insists that he also "resists dichotomization. . . . This is perhaps why it is difficult to locate the realm of the *caboclos* on the spirit-matter continuum."[21] That is, unlike the orixás, who manifest themselves in human bodies but are, as it were, *closed* themselves (they do not, for example, eat food, and, as I have emphasized, their motion is prescribed), the caboclos freely socialize, drink like fish, samba with people, and generally comport themselves like rude party animals.

One particularly interesting aspect of Wafer's book is that it also resists dichotomization. In a way, it is a long-overdue response to the ethnographic literature on the candomblé which has insufficiently addressed the role of gay men. Without explicitly representing itself as a book about homosexuality in Afro-Brazilian religion, *The Taste of Blood* counters the normative accounts of candomblé with one primarily peopled by men, and same-sex couplings are not marked in opposition to compulsory heterosexuality. Wafer espouses every form of "impurity": syncretic, sexual, and ethnographic.

I'm completely sympathetic to Wafer's project. It is true, however, that the majority of the more orthodox houses of candomblé—especially the nagô houses—are run and largely populated by women. Landes's celebratory title, *City of Women,* articulates a popular understanding of the power and privilege of women within Afro-Brazilian religion. The privileging of women's openness was a theme taken up, notably, by French feminist theorists in the '70s, and for Western readers of theory it is the notion of *écriture feminine* which will resonate with candomblé's view of privileged female sexuality. Hélène Cixous, in fact, invokes spirit possession in outlining female sexuality: "In the past, when carried to a rather spectacular degree, it was called 'possession.' Being possessed is not desirable for a masculine Imaginary, which would interpret it as passivity—a dangerous position."[22] Cixous acknowledges that historically women's "possession" has been linked to dispossession of the self, but she proposes an opening up of the self which might be not passive but expansive.

Such an expansion, she says, will be achieved through writing:

> I will say: today, writing is woman's. That is not a provocation, it means that woman admits there is an other. . . . It is much harder for man to let the other come through him. Writing is the passageway, the entrance, the exit, the dwelling place of the other in me—the other that I am and am not, that I don't know how to be, but that I feel passing, that makes me live— that tears me apart, disturbs me, changes me, who?—a feminine one, a masculine one, some?—several, some unknown, which is indeed what gives me the desire to know and from which all life soars. It is distressing, it wears you out; and for men this permeability, this nonexclusion is a threat, something intolerable.[23]

Cixous sees women's permeability as their openness to multifarious sexuality. A mother of saints might rather see her own permeability as an openness to Xangô, the thunder king—not an openness to his sexual penetration but to her own capacity to embody him.[24] But she is on similar ground with Cixous in seeing his choreography—the writing of the other *through her*— as the point of entry.

If in the preceding chapter I argued that samba rewrites the divine text of orixá choreography, I must give you—in a readable form—that text. Impossible! What follows might be seen as a description of the choreographies. But each one demonstrates the way in which, when the body's motion is *read* for divinity, the orixá embodies the erasure of the mimetic text. A reminder regarding context: these choreographies as standard versions of the dances are in their invocative forms. Divine presence—the descent of the god— always brings out the divinity's individuality. Each of us has her *own* orixá—when six Oguns descend at once, they are distinct, while the principle is transcendent. And as Maya Deren observed, the distinction of the orixá may be marked by virtuosity and innovation. In the invocative context, the dancers move slowly in a counterclockwise pattern. Reference here to direction must be understood as relative to the circular line of the overall direction of the group.

Generally, all orixá dance is initiated by an Exú choreography. Exú is not exactly an orixá but is the mercurial intermediary between us and them.[25] We dispatch him with a dance suggestive of a horse's gait, flexing at the knees, the arms cocked and slightly tensed but responsive to an invisible rein held in the fists. Occasionally the knees flex more deeply—this is called "breaking." The direction is vague, or rather unpredictable: the overall pattern, as I said, is counter-clockwise, but within that pattern the dancer can veer and turn in small tight circles in either direction. The difficulty in reading the dance gesturally, of course, is that the dancer appears to be both horse and rider. The choreography might be said to be evocative of Exú's ride to the realm of the gods, where we are sending him. But it might equally be seen as a reference to our own desire to be mounted—to serve, in Deren's words, divine horsemen. It is appropriate that this reading should fall somewhere between the physical and the divine, as this is where we locate—or fail to locate—Exú, who is always where we least expect him, here and there.

I have mentioned several aspects of Ogun's dance. In its use as invocation its moves are somewhat under-stated, but they are filled with potential. Danced to a 6/8, the lunging steps are made on the first and fourth beats. What would probably be perceived as the first downbeat of the rhythm is danced, however, as a pickup: the weight is lifted and suspended, shoulder blades drawn back, heels slightly off the ground. It is on the count of four, halfway through the measure, that the first heavy step forward, on a right diagonal, is made. Right, left, right—and again on the initial beat of the next phrase there is a lifting, a suspension of move-ment, and then the dancer lunges left, right, left on the other diagonal. The body is pitched forward, and on each step the arms make a snapped crossing gesture, the shoulder blades contracting between each osten-sible strike of the blade. But as I said earlier, there is no blade when we call on Ogun. Ogun is, as a principle, extreme materiality: iron. But our invocation to him is best when least material, when we do not turn our arms into a heavy-handed pantomime but gesture, precisely, the sword's absence. There are other moves: a triumphant dash forward, raising the arms overhead, then jerking back for several beats with the fists crossed over the chest and the head bowed; or a full-pitched sprint forward, snapping the arms crosswise, low, three times and then once over the head, repeatedly.

In the case of Ogun, how we read the gestures of the dance has to do with the physical object of the sword which the god will receive when he presents himself. The same is true of many of the orixás. When the lightning god Xangô descends, he is given his *xêrém, a* sacred rattle, and his thunderaxe. The thunderaxe looks like this:

The dance itself seems to draw the body up into a posture reminiscent of the axe: the shoulder blades again pull back, and the bent arms are lifted at almost right angles to the body. The motion of the upper body is a flashing one: the arms jerk up and down, the shoulders back and front. The feet, again on a 6/8 rhythm, fall in this pattern:

The small step on each third beat is a backward step, shifting the weight just long enough to let the body lunge even farther forward on the fourth beat. The lunging pattern is heavy, strong, and direct, while the upper body maintains its rapid flexing of the shoulders and skewed elbows. Do the arms represent the thunderaxe? The dance remains the same—in fact accrues violence and force—when Xangô arrives and takes up his literal axe. As a representation of the axe, the choreography would be redundant. It might be read, rather, as the action of manipulating the thunderaxe—and yet we know the axe is not an axe, but the nonphysical, insubstantial, but very potent electromagnetic phenomenon of lightning. The dance embodies the thing that cannot be materialized.

When Oxossi comes, he takes up a nonfunctional, fixed metal bow and arrow.

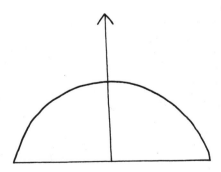

SAMBA

In invoking him, we hold our hands together, right thumb grasped in the left hand, right index finger extended like a dart in tension, waiting to be released. Oxossi, it has been suggested,[26] has taken on qualities of the hunt which were perhaps proper to Eyinlé (a separate divinity in Nigeria but a "quality" of Oxossi in Brazil) and Ogun in ancient Yoruba tradition. His dance, to a rhythm called *aguéré,* certainly resembles the *àgèrè* dance performed for Eyinlé and Ogun in Yorubaland today—although the finger-as-arrow is new. The feet—on a 4/4—take a step forward, back, and forward with the right (the left merely sliding slightly behind)—and then the weight shifts: left steps front, back, front, with the right sliding behind. When the right foot is stepping, the body is directed crosswise on a left diagonal, and vice versa. On the lifting beat just before the change in direction, the dancer often spins around full circle, to the back, such that her feet and the angle of her body are already in preparation for the next step. The spin requires an anticipation of the new path to be taken and an anticipatory focusing of energy which is akin to what is called "spotting" in Western dance. The posture is one of readiness, and the arms are tensed, dipping slightly as though searching their mark. Of course, the cocked finger would seem to be a physicalizing of the arrow. But neither the finger nor the literal arrow fused to its bow is functional. The principle of stealth escapes our own desire to embody it, until it embodies us.

Omolú, god of epidemics, can come down in two forms: as the old Omolú, awesome in his ancientness, or as young Obaluaiyé, all-powerful. His choreography is similar in both forms—it is the velocity of the dance which changes. Ancient Omolú's rhythm, *opanijé*, drags almost unbearably. It is extremely heavy, the sharp sticks slapping out a jagged beat that seems to trip over itself painfully. Omolú breaks at the knees, seeming always to be on the verge of collapse, bent nearly double. He steps on three heavily marked beats, dipping low, and then draws his feet together and reverses the pattern: right left right / left right left. When Omolú is present, the body is covered in raffia from head to toe, and he carries a flywhisk. Young Obaluaiyé particularly emphasizes the sweeping movement of the whisk. It has been read alternatively as spreading contagion or as sweeping it away.[27] When the whisk is not in hand, in the invocative dance, the hand itself makes the sweeping gesture. Omolú then breaks very low, almost falling headlong, or lunges to the left, arms raised in contortion, draws them back behind him, and spins low to the right, repeating the threat. Omolú, perhaps second only to Exú, is one of the most misunderstood of the orixás. Colonial authorities in Nigeria outlawed his worship, thinking his priests were intentionally spreading smallpox. To worship Omolú, or to dance for him, is not to pray for illness but to pray for an indication of the *meaning* of illness in the community. It is a question that can only be answered in pain and suspension: why do those we love fall ill and die? Omolú does not embody contagion. His gesture is unreadable because it cannot give a simple answer. His contortion is not the mere pain of smallpox, or, today, even AIDS. It is the pain of the community recognizing that the sickness of one belongs to us all. The prayer to recognize this is also a prayer for healing, not just of an individual's disease but also of his individuation and isolation among us.

Oxalá—purity and creativity—like Omolú may come down either young (Oxaguinhã) or old (Oxalufã). And like Omolú he flexes deeply at the knees. Oxalá is syncretized in Bahia with the city's patron saint, Our Lord of the Good End, a manifestation of Christ. He holds, when he descends in a body, an elaborate metal staff. When he dances, he supports his weight on the staff as he rocks on bent knees. Without the staff, in the invocation, the dancer cocks her arms slightly and moves them counter to the sway of her body, balancing her weight. The body rocks forward to the right, the right knee thrust out; she pulls back, straightening the knee, and rocks forward again, flexing. The feet shift slightly together, the dancer draws her weight up, and then begins again to the left. The dance might be perceived as miming a very old man's unsteady gait. But Oxaguinhã fills the dance with youthful potential. A couple of years ago, some very energetic kids taught me a hip-hop move which, I later realized, was precisely Oxalá's choreography. Which goes to show that the hipper you get, the more ancient you get. Which is exactly what Oxalá tells you.

While the choreographies of the male orixás, as I said, are read with reference to the metonymic, physical objects which they will receive on descending to this world, female orixás, who also receive accoutrements, tend rather to embody themselves surrounded by, and interacting with, their own principles. Yemanjá, for example, the goddess of salt waters, dances with a shimmering, shivering motion in the shoulders which resembles the sea's surface. Her ample arms outstretched, her ample breasts shaking with her fulsomeness, she steps forward and back on her right foot, the left nearly still, just skimming the surface on which she dances. She begins to pull her arms toward her in a gesture of collection: drawing her waters in as she does at low tide. Sometimes she bathes herself, scooping up the air-become-water which surrounds her and dousing herself in herself. In this sense she both *is* and *is in* water. Water in water disappears. But the principle of water makes herself manifest in the dance. It is impossible to fully literalize this principle *as* water, because an arm of water could not collect or contain itself.

Oxum, the goddess of fresh surface waters, is also the goddess of vanity and coquetry, and is perhaps the most self-reflexive of the orixás. She is in love with her own motion and cannot take her eyes off her image. When she comes down, she is given a brass fan (Yemanjá's is silver-colored), and a sword (Oxum is also a woman warrior). When she dances with these objects, she holds the fan at eye level and watches herself in it as though looking into a mirror. Oxum's rhythm is *ijexá*, a gentle 4/4. It is this rhythm which, with subtle changes in the bell part, becomes *afoxé*, the nonspecific rhythm to which all orixá choreographies are set in a secular context. Oxum steps delicately in a zigzag pattern on the heavy beats: right crosses slightly in front, left steps out; left crosses center and right steps out; and so on. Her hips sway, and her torso ripples gently with each step. One hand is extended, holding the sword, or if free it caresses her own hair and body,

SAMBA

as the other holds up her mirror. In the invocative version, the dancer holds up her own palm as the mirror. What does she see in this reflexive surface?[28] If the orixá is not present, the dancer of course can only see her own physicality. But this is not contradictory to Oxum, who is the principle of self-love and the embrace of one's own body. If Oxum is present, what can she see in the mirror? Only the physicality which is not herself in principle but in practice, except that the body incorporating Oxum becomes transcendentally beautiful.

The most celebrated mother of saints in Brazil in recent history was called Mãe Menininha, Mother Little Girl. Menininha (highly overrated in my own mother's magnificent estimation) inspired musical, literary, and visual tributes from many of Brazil's most renowned artists, including Jorge Amado and the poet-composers Dorival Caymmi, Vinícius de Moraes, Caetano Veloso, and Gilberto Gil. Every song, every poem, depicts Menininha in her embodiment of Oxum—quintessential gorgeousness! Never mind that she must have weighed in at a good four hundred pounds and wore thick eyeglasses. When she was with her Oxum, the goddess looked in the mirror and was delighted with her own image. The self-reflexive hand of the invocative choreography is and is not a mirror. It is a metaphor and a literalization—nonrepresentational, but real—of self-love. It is the principle made manifest in the material, but it invokes the principle herself to descend to embody it.

If Yemanjá collects water in her watery arms and Oxum reflects upon the idea of self-admiration, Iansã

similarly embodies and is surrounded by her own principle, which is the wind. At a furious pace, she steps
right left right / left right left, kicking up and out with her
wild flexed foot. Her hips fly loose, chaotic, in opposition to the feet, and open palms trace rapid, funneled
currents. The weight in this dance is constantly suspended, and performing it gives one the sense of
flight.[29] Iansã's suspension is not by any means indicative of weightlessness, and especially not powerless-
ness, as her transformative capacities are stunning.
More stunning still are those hips—site of her power,
her fire, source of frenzy and of her particular brand of
beauty.[30] Iansã's color is reddish brown, the color of
menstrual blood. She looks after women in childbirth,
in menstruation, in aborted pregnancy, and in meno-
pause. In a belief system which prizes human life and
fertility, she makes sure that birth will not take place
at the cost of the lives of women. Above all, her impossibly volatile hips seem to proclaim that women's
sexuality and reproductive rights belong to them. How
could a man contain this strength?

The motion of Iansã's dance, as I said, might be
read in reference to her association with windstorms.
And yet it is through the dancer's physicality—her
body in all its materiality, with the full weight of her
hips, her flesh and blood—that she creates a stir. This
dance is air and it is matter at once: the commotion of
pure directionality as it encounters the corporeal. The
fury of this clash is feminine, as it is women who so
often are forced to compromise their ideals with the
demands of and upon their bodies. When we dance to
call on Iansã, we set her in motion by calling on her as

a principle of belief—feminism—even as we bring her transcendental power down to the site of our repression—the body.

Still, we dance to accrue her power. There is another female orixá who comes down in order to warn us against her weakness. She is Obá. Earlier I mentioned the ostensible loss of many of the oral narratives in Brazil of the orixás. Obá's choreography would seem not to be a replacement of her story but rather a reinforcement or reminder of it. Obá's pathetic little story is the kind that never stops circulating, that fascinates us as we pray not to reproduce it. She is the negative image of Iansã and Oxum—disempowered by her sex, submissive and self-sacrificing. The story goes that Obá was a less-favored wife of Xangô. Iansã, despite her "difficult" personality—or because of it—delighted Xangô, as did Oxum, for clearly different reasons. Like all gossip, this story has different versions, some indicating Iansã as the deceptive, favored wife, and some indicating Oxum. What we do know is that Obá, mealy-mouthed and too eager to please, asked one of these two for her secret in satisfying their husband. Her co-wife took no pity but rather offense at Obá's meekness, and told her a terrible lie: our husband loves a special soup—cut off your ear and cook it in the broth. Obá did it, and Xangô ate the soup. When he found the strange brown shriveled mushroom at the bottom of the bowl, he asked what it was. Obá lifted her head-cloth and showed him the wound of her adoration. Xangô was disgusted. Who could love Obá?

Or, maybe you are wondering, why do we worship her? Female servitude is self-confounding, ugly, pathetic. We call her down because we need to be re-minded. When Obá arrives, she moves in humiliation and contraction. But what most marks her dance is her hand, shameful, covering her severed ear. The dancer who invokes her, of course, covers an uncut ear. The choreography, that is, is a double concealment: it hides the fact that the dancer is not a literalization of Obá, who would be hiding not an ear but a wound. When Obá is actually incorporated in the dance, what does she hide behind her hand? To answer this is to under-stand the other moral behind Obá's story: one *cannot* overliteralize with the body. Obá's desire to be self-sacrificing was made manifest when she cut off her ear. Horrible error! When we read the orixá choreogra-phies, we have to be reminded of this. Readings of the dances which see them as mere pantomimes of divine principles are too literal-minded. The dancing body, as it calls upon divinity, embodies its own unreadability.

There are, finally, a few orixás of indeterminate gender. Ossãe, god of herbalism, Oxumaré, the rainbow serpent, and Logun-édé, offspring of Oxossi and Oxum, are all hermaphroditic, either divided between the top and bottom halves of their "bodies" or divided tempo-rally, spending six months of each year as male, then female. Ossãe appears most frequently of the three, and when her/his dance is performed, the dancer spins and hops on one foot, marking the god's mutilation: Ossãe perches over leaves on one leg like a bird, blinking a single eye, squeaking out a song with a laryn-gitic voice. It has been suggested that bodily damage—all this halving of parts—was a result of Ossãe's jeal-ousy in guarding herbal secrets.[31] Wafer offers another suggestion: that Ossãe's long raffia costume hides a different wounding—the sexual defilement of the king of the forest by Oxossi, hunter-rapist.[32] Interestingly, all of the orixás held to be of split gender are associated with the forces of the bush: they are particular friends of the caboclos.[33]

All of the dances I've written of here are meaningless until the orixá comes down. They are a prayer for significance. I said that the secular interpretations of the dances in the afoxés were, precisely, literalizations—they would be too narrative, too mimetic in the context of orixá invocation in the candomblé. But I must say (sorry, Mother) I find them beautiful, because they also call on, invoke, significance. The afoxés invoke political significance and embody aesthetic power.

To say that the afoxés call for social justice is to say, in the terms of the candomblé, that they invoke Xangô. To say they celebrate an aesthetic tradition as a means to achieve political power is to invoke seductive Oxum as woman warrior. To acknowledge that this tradition is one largely carried out by women on the strength of their strained backs and in the burden of their bellies is to invoke Iansã. To say these rhythms are contagious is to invoke the power of Omolú. African textuality has certainly been displaced in many ways in Brazil. Afoxé dances attempt actively to inscribe the stories of the orixás. But the bodies of the dancers become inscribed into these stories. And even here, my own writing is absorbed by the orixá principles which I could only have learned through dance. Writing, in fact, has become so dispersed, so physicalized, that even the simplest gesture is described as such. Some Bahians call eating with the hands "manuscrito"—manuscript. To eat with the hands might be perceived as a sign of humiliation. But it is how food is eaten in the candomblé, as a reminder of servitude not to men, never to men, but to the gods. As we eat, we are both eating and writing our rice and beans. And food tastes better when it is significant!

We were sitting in the kitchen in the *terreiro,* the compound of the orixás, all of us dressed in white. I had to sit on the floor all that day, marking my humility before the gods and my commitment to the ground, the ground to which I had pressed my head in supplication, on which I had danced the night before for hours in obligation, which had absorbed the blood of my sacrifices. I was sitting on the ground and there were small children next to me and I felt myself a child although I was a woman. My mother of saints was eating with her fingers, she had a yellow streak of palm oil around her mouth—oily, sensual mouth. We were eating with our fingers, simplest thing, we ate the sacrificed roosters, bony, gristled, blessed food. My mother was laughing, remembering my dancing the night before—I pleased her. Little Lumidé, six years old, luminously beautiful, besides my mother of saints was my best teacher. Aildes told her to show me something: Yemanjá's proper collection of the waters. Priestess of the goddess of the sea, Lumidé in her tiny black body, shining in her tiny white dress, stood, her

SAMBA

little fingers and mouth still glistening with oil, her little black eyes glistening, and danced with perfect simplicity. Six! She knew every choreography, and sometimes received Yemanjá.

How can such a tiny body hold so much fulsomeness—hold the principle of oceans? Each of us is a small child, fragile, vulnerable. Our bodies collect potential—axé—when we call into them a significance which will always exceed the individual capacities of both motion and imagination. Mother Aildes would stroke that tiny head lovingly: "a pretinha linda do candomblé"—beautiful little black girl of the candomblé. Lumidé was fulsome in her black luminousness—in understanding herself as the daughter of the house, the embodiment of the past, the future of the candomblé. Little teacher, I am trying to learn your lessons, to dance with significance, to see how small yet fertile with meaning I might be.

My own orixás are Oxum and Iansã as my mother read them in the *búzios,* or cowrie shells of Ifá. This may explain a few things—my luxurious exhibitionism in Mother Aildes's receiving room, for example, or in any roda de samba; my self-reflexivity; my weakness for what's gawdy, sparkly, or lyrical. And on the side of Iansã, my abhorrence of the unjust suffering of women. Aildes was a priestess of Iansã, and I told her I aspired to her strength and spontaneity. She had no fear of blood! She told me I would get there, and it is this tremendous hope that is riding on these hips when I let them loose, like a whirlwind. *Ora-iéié-ô, Oxum. Éparrei, Iansã.* These are the salutations we cry to my orixás when they come down. They can *only* come down in their choreographies, their own writing. As what you read now is *my* writing, it can't contain divinity. But each time we attempt to serve a principle—of self-reflexive lyricism or feminism, for example—we are being written by the orixás, and in this sense we embody them. It is not an imitation of the orixás but an offering to them.

The only meaningful human writing, as I have come to see it, is done in the service of belief. This may not be articulated as belief in the orixás but as belief in political or aesthetic principles. Precisely. I am trying to feel my mind work like a muscle.

SAMBA

Samba: the body articulate.
Photo by B. Browning.

Divine choreography.
Photo by Andy Young.

SAMBA

Invocative dance in the
candomblé.
Photo by Andy Young.

Axé increasing in the
counterclockwise circle.
Photo by Andy Young.

SAMBA

Benção: capoeira's ironic blessing.
Photo by Chris Davis.

Capoeira in Central Park.
Photo by Chris Davis.

SAMBA

Loremil Machado: the metaphysical
cartwheel.
Photo by Chris Davis.

Rehearsal of an afoxé.
Photo by B. Browning.

SAMBA

Dance of the chicken.
Photo by B. Browning.

Inventing new moves in the
carnaval.
Photo by B. Browning.

More carnaval moves.
Photo by B. Browning.

83

SAMBA

The notorious Apaches.
Photo by Osmar Gama.

Choreographing gender.
Photo by Osmar Gama.

3. Headspin: Capoeira's Ironic Inversions

Despite my mother of saints' warnings, I continue to hang with capoeiristas, even here in New York. My mãe de santo would shake her head and curl her lip: "They're dirty, they're womanizers, and they're always up to no good." But when someone struck the chord on a *berimbau,* even she would get a sly look, sway a bit tentatively from side to side, then swat at the unsuspecting air with her cocked foot. "I know a thing or two . . ." Somebody taught her this, and knowing her, I wouldn't be surprised if she'd deigned to get pretty familiar with some elegant ruffian along the way.

Capoeira's elegance is excruciating, its seductive capacities never to be underestimated. But a capoeirista never stays still for long, which is why it's dangerous to set your heart on holding him in one place. A few years ago I had a friend named Wilson dos Santos. He'd written a screenplay about himself called "Capoeirista in New York." It was mostly a true story, embellished with some high-powered fight scenes. Wilson dreamed of doing for capoeira, the Afro-Brazilian dance and martial art, what Bruce Lee did for kung fu. When he was a scrappy, restless kid, a beach urchin in Bahia, he got into some scuffles. There's a thin keloid remembrance of the tip of a knife near his nipple, another on his arm. But once he made up his mind to get to the United States and make it as a performer, he gave up all that and began to think of himself as a dancer. He stayed here in New York for a few years, disappeared to Los Angeles, and ended up in Las Vegas doing acrobatics on a casino stage. Wilson had two looks. One was when his face would fill up with a childlike uncontrollable exuberance, his smile all teeth, and he was liable to go bounding off in a series of flips. The other was when he'd slip on his dark glasses, plug into his Walkman, and tuck into his stride. He had a small brown body like a clenched fist.

Capoeirista in New York—that was me, too, and I played the part: my friends and I used to stride through the park leonine and muscular, feeling the mechanism of our bodies walking, and the material presence of the sun on our shoulders. The first capoeiristas in New York were Jelon Vieira and Loremil Machado, and they arrived in 1975. Old friends, they had utterly different personalities, and their games showed it. Jelon is massive, solid as a rock, and his capoeira is stonily intimidating. It's only when he cracks a shy smile that you get a glimpse at his tremendously tender part. Loremil had a small, agile body of incomparable finesse and almost unbearable charm. He was constantly goofing, his game loaded with humor. He never "fought" a match but played with the pure joy of a child discovering the freedom of motion. It was only rarely that you glimpsed his real strength: the flexible but accurate, piercing arrow of Oxossi. Jelon has taught many Americans to play capoeira, and has inspired in all of them a quiet, profound respect. Loremil's effect on people was different: mad, aching, passionate love.

I knew Loremil for ten years, and I suppose I loved him as achingly as I'll ever love anybody. But all of his friends and students, however much time they spent with him, say he taught them this: how to throw themselves headlong into the pleasure of having a body. When he passed away a few months ago, forty years old, as childlike and innocent as ever, I think this is what hurt us most: the thought of his having to leave behind a body that he enjoyed so intensely. But maybe that last maneuver was just the ultimate acrobatic stunt—a cartwheel into a world of *truly* free motion.

Capoeira is a game, a fight, and a dance, composed of kicks, acrobatics, and traditional Kongo dance movements. One doesn't speak of "dancing" or "fighting" capoeira but rather of "playing": *jogar capoeira.*[1] Or one can eliminate the substantive and use the simple verb *vadiar*: to bum around. And yet capoeiristas universally take the game very seriously. Most, when asked to define it in a word, call it an art.[2] In New York I once saw a capoeirista wearing a button that said "Doing strange things in the name of art." And it's true, they will go to extremes.

While some people will tell you there are two basic styles of capoeira,[3] there are in fact as many as there are great capoeiristas. But certain generalizations apply. Capoeira is always played in a *roda*—the same circle formation that delimits all traditional Afro-Brazilian dance. Two players enter the roda at a time, and their focus remains on each other, while they may pivot either clockwise or counterclockwise throughout the game. Motion is generally circular. Kicks and sweeps are more often than not arched or spinning, and they loop together in a series of near misses. The ideal is to keep one's eyes fixed on one's opponent. At times this necessitates having eyes in the back of one's head. But the relative placement of body parts or facial features seems to be constantly ridiculed anyway. The capoeirista spends a good deal of time inverted, with hands planted firmly like feet on the ground, feet slapping happily like palms in the air. The upside-down face, like those magical cartoons from our childhood where the hair became a beard and the creased forehead a smirking, lipless mouth, grins at your attempts to fix it. And still, those eyes are on you.

How do I reconcile this silly picture with what I want to communicate of capoeira's elegance and even gravity? The game can be humorous, but it is not self-ridiculing—at least not simply so. This is partly because of the obvious physical prowess involved, but even more because of the understanding of the role of capoeira in popular histories.

As usual, a linear history of capoeira is far from satisfactory. The popular histories which circulate most commonly seem to pit forces of influence against each other in a struggle for control of the game: African versus European or Asian values and gestural vocabularies, ruffianism versus links to the military police, tradition versus corruption, chaos versus discipline. Depending on one's perspective, these influences may seem to be playing out a struggle between good and evil. But capoeira, whatever one's style or perspective, always ironizes the notion of Manichean extremes. Just when you think you've determined who are the good and the bad, it all suddenly strikes you rather as an aesthetic issue, excepting that you can't tell anymore what is ugly and what is beautiful. And an upside-down mug is grinning at you, pug-ugly, gorgeous.

Nobody generally "wins" a game of capoeira—although in recent years there have sprung up various tournaments and other events—but that's all part of the story. There are takedowns, and certainly the ability to apply them effectively adds to one's prestige as a capoeirista. But gratuitous, unprovoked violence or even humorless humiliation of one's opponent (or partner?) is never admired. The question is at what point provocation occurs. In a tight, "inside" game (*jogo de dentro*) when the players are interweaving spinning kicks, the agility and precision of one opens a precise space for the elegant partnering of the other. But there may be a moment imperceptible to a spectator when somehow synchronicity shatters and there are in fact two opposing forces. Someone provoked. Someone sprung malice, which was always inherent in the moves.

However they have developed, the question of where these moves originated is one that inspires impassioned arguments from most capoeiristas. Capoeira is decidedly an Afro-Brazilian art, but which half of this term should be weighted? The simplest little narrative in circulation is something like this: prior to their captivity and enslavement in Brazil, the people of the Kongo-Angola region practiced certain kicking games for sport and recreation. In Brazil, the games were prohibited for all too obvious reasons. But the Kongo people continued practicing their games in seclusion. The roda was formed as a protective circle, and the choreographic elements—as well as music—were added to disguise a fight as a dance. Repression of the practice continued even after abolition. The players invented a special rhythm, *cavalaria,* an imitation of the sound of approaching horses' hooves, to warn each other of police surveillance, and on that cue the capoeira became an "innocent" samba. In other words, capoeiristas generally acknowledge that a martial arts technique and choreographic and rhythmic vocabularies were brought from Africa. But the strategic blending of fight and dance occurred in Brazil, under specific pressures. And while this strategy appears to have been directed against forces outside the roda de capoeira, it became the fundamental strategy *within* the game. Dance—as seduction, illusion, deception— became dangerous, and kicks became elements of choreography. The Portuguese tolerated the roda de capoeira because it was merely dance—perceived as motion without purpose or effect, other than aesthetic. And within the circles, Africans in Brazil trained like fighters in the art of dissimulation—how to grin upside down.

This story is typical of those recounted in the capoeira community—although there are variations placing greater and lesser emphasis on tradition or change, on Africanness or Brazilianness. Ethnographic narratives of origin also vary, although the most powerful arguments come from scholars who view themselves as advocates of African diasporic culture. Righteously countering centuries of European dismissal of sophisticated African traditions, scholars like Robert Farris Thompson, Kenneth Dossar, and Gerhard Kubik[4] have given a strong case for the ever-fresh inscription of Kongo cosmology in capoeira's designs. I find these arguments powerful not simply because of their convincing "evidence" but because of their commitment to the principles of resistance which are at the heart of capoeira.

More politicized capoeiristas in Brazil also tend to emphasize African sources. If the seeds of the game existed in Angola but the intention or strategy developed in Brazil, then it would appear that capoeira must be acknowledged as an authentically Afro-Brazilian form. But when black nationalist Brazilians regard capoeira as an African form, their argument is strong. If one recognizes that Bahia, the capital of capoeira and Afro-Brazilian culture generally, resembles a West African port city much more than it does any city in Latin America, the gap of the Atlantic begins to seem quite incidental. The historical fact of forced migration is not forgettable, but the racial and cultural constituency of Bahia is overwhelmingly African. The dance forms which developed there were influenced by Europeans and indigenous Brazilians, but they developed in a culturally African metropolis.

Gestural vocabularies, as I noted, are difficult to trace, so arguments regarding the history of capoeira frequently rest on linguistic etymologies. The etymological debate has been characterized by one historian as "a linguistic version of antiquarian disputes over empirical details in history."[5] There is something oddly literal-minded about this line of research, considering that capoeira's own strategy is founded on irony: saying one thing and meaning another. Capoeira, like samba, is an alternative language to the dominant one. Gerhard Kubik[6] suggests a Bantu derivation of the term, and given the general acceptance of the largely Kongo-Angolan roots of the game, it's surprising this argument hasn't gained greater currency. But etymological hypotheses are also narratives, and they have political significances.

In contemporary usage, the word *capoeira* refers most often to the game, but there are two other meanings in standard Brazilian Portuguese: bush and chicken coop. The latter meaning derives from the Portuguese word *capão*, which means rooster and is related to the English word *capon*. Some suggest that the game resembled a chicken fight, the scrambling of two birds in a cage. Whether the term would have been applied in this case by Portuguese observing the practice or ironically by capoeiristas themselves is not clear. Another suggestion is that the chicken coop label was attached metonymically rather than metaphorically: it was the Africans taking fowl to sell at the markets who practiced the game in public plazas, transferring the name of their merchandise to their pastime.

Capoeira as "bush," or wild space, is said to derive from Tupi roots (*caá*: forest, *puêra*: extinct). Again, the etymology may be "true" or "false"—although its accuracy is less interesting than the association of a term for wildness with the indigenous Brazilian. As I suggested in the previous chapters and will develop further in the next, the figure of the "Indian" or caboclo absorbs wilderness from both Portuguese and African imaginations in Brazil. While no explicit connection is indicated between indigenous games or dances and capoeira, the caboclo figure bears certain similarites to the capoeirista. As I have written, the caboclo is an emblem in Afro-Brazilian culture of the refusal to be or remain a captive. One popular conception of capoeira is that it was developed as a means of self-defense for slaves hoping to escape to independent black communities in the backlands of the agricultural states. These communities, *quilombos,* have been documented as remarkably developed urban centers with organized political and market systems.[7] The best known was called Palmares, in the interior of the state of Alagoas. Capoeiristas insist that it was the art of capoeira which defended Palmares against repeated attempts to dismantle it and return its residents to captivity.

The efficiency of capoeira in defending a community against mounted, armed invasions is questionable, and this part of the story may well have been inflated over the years.[8] Brazilian director Carlos Diegues's 1984 film, *Quilombo*, showed highly romanticized scenes of young boys practicing cartwheels in training for the defense of their society. But to return to the etymological significance of the bush, the wild place, the caboclo's terrain—one thing should be mentioned. Capoeira is an urban phenomenon. It has always flourished in high-density areas: Salvador, Bahia; possibly Palmares; New York City. The urban bush. The notion of its wildness, even the animality of its motion, doesn't mean it came organically from an uncivilized, un-Europeanized space. It was constructed specifically to counter European pressures.

Most capoeiristas and historians are in agreement on most of the details of this account of capoeira's origin. But its consequent developments are contested. The roda de capoeira ostensibly began as a protective circle enclosing the capoeiristas who were in training— in the process of an organized transmission of techniques of resistance. But capoeira's bright image as a system of righteous defense becomes confused in the eighteenth century with boundless, undirected, or uncontrolled violence. In the major cities, gangs known as *maltas*, largely composed of mixed-race, impoverished free men, we are told,[9] used capoeira technique in general looting and gang fighting. Under such circumstances, they dispensed with the roda, as well as the dance.

This is the beginning of capoeira's association with ruffianism—an association which continued to have currency, to varying degrees, over the years. But the idea of breaking out of boundaries, of getting out of control, is not only figured in the broken circle, the shattered roda where dance explodes into class unrest and violence. Ostensibly, racial borders as well were being broken. The so-called *mulato* capoeirista is a figure moving between categories. He exists at the anxious point of contact between blacks and whites. And while that point of contact was sexualized in the body of the *mulata* sambista, it is made violent in that of the capoeirista. In fact (as is the case with the crack sambistas as well), while they may be narrated as embodying the mixture of races, capoeiristas are in the majority black. But in the period immediately preceding and following slavery's abolition in 1888, they absorbed some of the racial fears of a society in transition.

The music stopped—at least on the soundtrack of the romanticized, cinematic version of the story. But there is something suspect in the suggestion that the intention of capoeira had essentially changed. Was it a black dance when contained within the roda, when it expressed self-irony, restricted to black-on-black aggression? Even on the quilombos, the roda de capoeira as a training ground for defense seems ultimately unthreatening to white authority, because it is isolated. The quilombos were remarkably successful, but basically self-contained. That may be what allows for their romanticization in retrospect: Palmares has come to represent a never-never land where racial injustice didn't have to be dealt with as long as there was minimal contact with white society.

During the "ruffian" stage, it's said that capoeira was still occasionally played in the "old style"—as a dance, a game, a diversion. But this qualitative difference may not have been so much a change in style or form as a change in perspective and context. Capoeira, however dissimulating, has always held violent potential. It has also long maintained an ambiguous relationship to white authority. In the early nineteenth century, at the start of Dom João VI's monarchy, the first official police force was instituted in Brazil, and the head of the Royal Guard, a Major Vidigal, is supposed to have been a powerful capoeirista. He is also supposed to have been charged with keeping the ruffian capoeira contingent in line.

Capoeiristas were absorbed into the order during the brief war with Paraguay in 1865. They were forcibly recruited and are said to have fought valiantly. A number of traditional capoeira song lyrics refer to this event. The capoeiristas returned to the cities of Salvador and Rio with renewed prestige, although the situation was short-lived. When the roda, the circle of control, could not be maintained, capoeira was again perceived as a threat. The Penal Code of 1890 legislated corporal punishment or forced exile for the practitioners of capoeira. Even early in this century, according to the great fighter Master Bimba,

> the police persecuted a capoeirista like you chase after a damn dog. Just imagine, one of the punishments they gave capoeiristas that were caught playing was to tie one wrist to a horse's tail, and the other to another horse. The two horses were sent running toward the police station. We even used to make a joke, that it was better to play *near* the police station, because there were many cases of death. The individual couldn't support being pulled at high velocity along the ground and died before arriving at his destination.[10]

SAMBA

But it was Bimba, in fact, who initiated certain changes so that, in time, capoeira began to be tolerated as a game—under certain circumstances. It was more or less institutionalized. And you still find in Brazil the popular conception that street capoeira is for trouble-makers, and the only respectable place for the game is in the capoeira "academies."

If the joke was that it was better to play near the police station, the academicization of capoeira in some ways realized such an approximation. The academy became the controlled space. It was a structure of containment, not a protective circle like the roda. And yet ostensibly the academy serves the function of an educational space. Politicized black parents today send their children to capoeira academies to learn about their cultural heritage.

As an initiate in the U.S. "academy," I am always particularly interested in notions of pedagogy in the Afro-Brazilian context. The "alternative" pedagogical institution may appear to be a simple ironic response to dominant, repressive, or exclusionary institutions: the capoeira academy in opposition to the police academy, or the samba school in opposition to an educational system which denies the cultural validity of one's African heritage. But it isn't that simple. The phrase *escola de samba* is popularly held to derive from the schoolyard location of the first group's early rehearsals. That metonymic explanation doesn't preclude irony, but the Rio samba schools can't really be held up as shining examples of antihegemonic, popular education.[11] The twitching white soap-opera star who crowns a Rio carnaval float is the same schoolmarm as that of the national broadcast which portrays whiteness as desirability. The lesson is the same. The capoeira academies also reiterate, sometimes, rigid, linear pedagogical technique which seems bought wholesale from the police academy. Still, there *are* valuable lessons of African history and aesthetics. I take all this to heart as an educator who attempts to transmit non-Western culture through historically Eurocentric institutions.[12] Certainly the *way* we read, teach, and write about culture is as important as the particular manifestations we're considering. The capoeira academies demand that we rethink inclusion and exclusion, cultural containment and liberational pedagogy.

When Bimba instituted his academy, he modified not only the vocabulary of capoeira but also its mode of transmission. Bimba was born Manoel dos Reis Machado, about a decade after abolition. His nickname, which means "little boy's dick," was applied at birth by the midwife who delivered him. As a child he studied capoeira with an African shipper who worked in the bay. But in 1932 he founded a school for a practice he called "a luta regional baiana"—Bahian regional wrestling. What he called this activity is a matter of particular interest to those who subsequently took issue with Bimba's teachings. The game he developed came to be called *capoeira regional* and is now usually regarded as one of the two principal styles of capoeira—and certainly the most popular. In distinction, another style, which is generally regarded as more traditional, became specified as *capoeira angola*.

SAMBA

Today the *angoleiros,* or practitioners of the "old" style, sometimes argue that regional isn't even capoeira. They point to the name Bimba first gave it as evidence. This position has been reinforced by the Brazilian ethnographic community, which, as usual, is unimpressed by the apparent absorption of non-African influences into Afro-Brazilian forms. In a 1975 work on capoeira, Edison Carneiro reduces regional to a dismissive paragraph:

> The capoeirista Bimba, a virtuoso on the *berimbau* [the main instrument of capoeira music], became well-known when, in the 1930s, he created a school for the training of athletes in the so-called Bahian regional wrestling, a mixture of capoeira with ju-jitsu, boxing and tag. Popular, folkloric capoeira, the legacy of Angola, has little, almost nothing to do with Bimba's school.[13]

The young capoeiristas today who opt for an orthodox angola style are disinclined to acknowledge regional as having anything to do with capoeira. And they keep pointing to that name—a luta regional baiana—as evidence.

But this preoccupation with nomenclature again strikes me as misguided considering that capoeira's foundation is one of dissimulation. Capoeira has always been a fight. Calling it a game or a dance has never detracted from the fact that Africans in Brazil developed it with the potential to disarm whites, whether through literal blows or through the subtle art of seeming to be in meaningless motion while actually reinforcing a circle of cultural and political race consciousness.

In fact, the angola-regional division is much less clear-cut than it may seem. Following the terminology

of a contemporary master, John Lowell Lewis has identified a third, synthetic rubric: *capoeira atual*, or current,
up-to-date capoeira.[14] As I have said, capoeira styles
vary greatly from one master to the next. If the whole
premise of the game is not to block one's opponent
but rather to take his movement in and invert it, then
it's easy to see how apparently differing styles could be
absorbed and modified by each other. It gets even
more complicated than that. Lewis suggests that in
recent years, the increased interest in capoeira angola
in Brazil might have been spurred by the enthusiasm of
black players from the United States, who studied the
regional style at home and then went to Brazil to find
an expression of African roots. Their "discovery" of the
funkier version may have influenced Brazilian players'
perspectives on angola.[15] Lewis suggests that regional
expressed a drive for "modernization," while capoeira
atual might be seen as a postmodern expression.
This observation highlights several interesting features
of contemporary capoeira: its temporal alinearity (such
that what's oldest appears most up-to-date); its en-
tanglement in global cultural exchange (such that U.S.
players may have encouraged Brazilians to reject extrinsic influences which have "contaminated" regional);
and its indecipherable self-irony (such that it's impossible to say if capoeira atual is angola goofing
on regional, or vice versa). But then again, all these
riddles—temporal, cross-cultural, self-ironic—are what
we have been reading as central to capoeira from its
very origins.

If capoeira was repressed during the historical
period when its expression of racial tension became too
clear, Bimba in a sense was deploying a very orthodox

capoeira strategy in remasking the game not as an "Angolan" art but as a regional, Bahian one. The new name smacked of local political savvy—call it not only Brazilian but Bahian. It doesn't sound like African nationalism or black consciousness, unless one suggests, as I did earlier, that many cultural developments in Bahia, seen from an African nationalist perspective, *are* African.

But Bimba's reforms went further than the name. Carneiro is accurate in saying that he added moves from Asian martial arts as well as U.S. boxing to capoeira's vocabulary. One of Bimba's students has argued:

> Mestre Bimba was accused of introducing into Capoeira movements from other martial arts. He laughed at this criticism but on several occasions admitted he had used attacks and defenses from boxing and ju-jitsu. One who did not know anything about Capoeira could easily have taken these statements literally. However, I believe that Mestre Bimba only adopted this stance to bring the prestige of foreign arts to Capoeira in order to attract more students.[16]

When the angoleiros dismiss these modifications on style as being "not real capoeira," they are arguing for something more important than the maintenance of a tradition. If capoeira is regarded as historical evidence of black resistance, they want to show that African forms are in themselves valid, durable and effective weapons. This is doubtless true. But if part of the genius of African religion in Brazil is syncretism, its ability to absorb or account for Catholic or other systems, part of capoeira's genius has also been its ability to absorb rather than be displaced by other forms. It is a survival tactic consistent with the premise of the game.

Locating what is "really" African in Brazilian culture is, as I have argued in the preceding chapters, not a simple project of mapping surface continuities. Much more interesting is the continuity of strategies for cultural survival. Of course, this argument itself is a tricky maneuver. It's what allows Bimba—and his student—to give two accounts of the sources of capoeira regional. Bimba "laughed at" the charges of foreign influences. He also "admitted" drawing on U.S. and Asian techniques. His student tells us not to take the statements (which ones?) literally, because they were strategic—and the strategy is recognizable to anyone who is familiar with the strategy of the game. In other words, the apparent contradiction is resolved by the fact that the very strategy of appropriating extrinsic movements is intrinsic to capoeira. The larger argument is that the very strategy of appropriating extrinsic culture is intrinsic to African culture. There is obviously a downside to this line of reasoning: one loses sight of the abundant clear and stunning manifestations of powerful traditions which mark themselves as African not only in evasive strategy but also in outright, dignified cultural and political reference. A proud angoleiro who calls his game by its African name makes a powerful statement. Centrifugal and centripetal forces act upon each other. Neither tells the truer story: they are both necessary and perhaps complementary strategies.

Bimba was a jet black Brazilian. The majority of his students were white. Some were members of the same police force that in his youth rounded up outlaw capoeiristas. Bimba's style of teaching was based on a notion of discipline. The rigorous control of his academy so impressed local political figures that he was invited to make presentations at the governor's palace in Bahia and, in 1953, before the president of the republic, Getúlio Vargas. After this demonstration, Vargas announced that "Capoeira is the only true national sport."[17] The path was open for official acceptance, and this had as much to do with Bimba's disciplinary example as it did with his athletic prowess. Bimba's teaching method entailed a classification of movements and the training of "sequences"—choreographed exchanges between partners. The sequences are symmetrical: kicks and ducks are trained equally on each side. The first partner executes a series of kicks with the second responding with the "correct" defenses, and then offensive/defensive roles are switched.

Politicized angoleiros generally seem much more critical of Bimba's bringing white *moves* into the roda than they are of his bringing in white students. But it is even rarer to hear an angoleiro complain about Bimba's methodology—his introduction of a linear, sequential mode of instruction into a quintessentially circular form. This may be because they recognize that different organizational principles may be helpful or even necessary for political mobilization. The protective roda has been a charged space for cultural transmission and creativity. But determined linearity has its advantages for activism. Bimba's relation to the political authorities was complex: even as he was embraced by them, he depicted himself as a rogue. And even those who reject regional as a style seem to respect his personal resistance.

In Bimba's academy, individual progress was marked by the *formatura*, or graduation ceremony. The students would demonstrate their skills in pairs, until the moment of the "orator's" speech. The orator was an advanced and particularly articulate student who would be called on to recount some of capoeira's history, as well as the accomplishments of the master. A small medal and a silk scarf were handed to the "godmother" accompanying each student. A blue scarf signified completion of the course. The scarf, according to Bimba, was a reminder of the old-time rogue capoeiristas who wore silk around their throats to thwart the razor's cut. Then each student would have to execute correctly a series of moves, and finally prove himself in the game by completing a match without "dirtying his clothes"— a euphemism for falling on one's ass.

Many academies today operate on a "cord" system resembling the belt system of Asian martial arts. The cord is strung around the waist, or through the belt loops of the *abadá,* a pair of regulation white pants. But different groups have designated different color codes—some based on the colors of the Brazilian flag, some based on the colors associated with the orixás. Formaturas—full graduations which constitute something like teacher accreditation—are much less common today than *batizados,* or baptisms, which simply mark intermediate stages of progress. At most batizados, the students are given nicknames (*nomes de guerra*— literally, war names) according to some personal peculiarity. They then get the baptismal dunking: a patronizing match with a superior player, concluding with a supremely humiliating sweep. The batizado, like the benção, is of course another clever turn on Catholic ceremony. The dunking is not in water but in earth, and the affected part is more likely the ass than the head. But in a more serious vein, the player is ceremonially brought to that liminal place that divides the sacred and the profane, the immortal and the mortal: the ground. Bimba instituted academic training, but now many angoleiros subscribe to the ceremonial marking of progress toward a goal. And perhaps the marking of individual progress is just part of a larger acceptance of the benefit of marking progress toward communal goals. Of course, as usual, one moves forward by getting closer to the ground of one's ancestral past.

There is another great figure in capoeira's modern history who is usually discussed in counterdistinction to Mestre Bimba, and he is the old-time angoleiro Mestre Vicente Ferreira Pastinha. Whereas Bimba was a large, bolt-upright, barrel-chested man, Pastinha was tiny and slight. At the end of his life he was blind and stooped, and in the late photographs, he seems to be swallowed up by his baggy clothing and the mashed-up old hat on his head. His big dim useless eyes had an expression of exquisite tenderness, despite a curious half-smile. My mother of saints said, "Ha! Everybody thinks Pastinha was such a sweet little guy. I knew him and he was a woman-user and a dirty, manipulative son of a bitch like the rest of them." I believe it, though that doesn't mean I don't love the idea of him. A woman friend and I were looking at one of his last snapshots: fragile, bent over playing capoeira music, the stick of the berimbau pressing into his tiny thigh. His miniature feet seem lost in their oversized sandals; the cuffs of his trousers are rolled up to show two rickety little ankles. "But look at his dick!" said my friend. There it is in the folds of cloth, unmistakable: the dick of Exú, divine engorged rod of mischief.

Angola speaks softly and carries a big stick. The style of the game is much less apparently aggressive than regional. The angoleiro wreaks havoc not through his powerful athleticism, as does the regionalista, but through the subtle art of *malícia*, which doesn't translate as malice, really, so much as street smarts, or cunning. It is the art of irony, Exú's domain, and the roda is the circle within which all words have doubled meanings. Even no means yes.

Pastinha's teachings are passed on by angoleiros with reverence. But in contrast to Bimba's directives, Pastinha's aphorisms, inscribed in a little book he wrote and recorded on an LP, sound like riddles. He went around planting these seeds of confusion. Bira Almeida opens his book on capoeira with one:

> Once I asked the wise Mestre Vicente Ferreira Pastinha—what is Capoeira, Mestre? "Capoeira is whatever the mouth eats."[18]

Almeida goes on to describe Pastinha's extinguished eyes, his soft voice, his tattered little world, and confesses, with hushed respect, "I did not understand his answer." No kidding.

Most everything Pastinha said is lyrical and indecipherable. But his ambiguity isn't without significance. It's strategic lyricism. Much of Pastinha's philosophy is embedded in the lyrics of capoeira songs that he sang.

SAMBA

Most capoeira standards are ancient, passed on by generations of nameless players. But the great masters mark themselves by self-referentiality into songs, or by creating images so powerful that a particular lyric is indelibly associated with them. Capoeira songs generally express the ambiguity of the game, and the most obvious example is this simple call and response pattern: "Oi sim sim sim, Oi não não não"—oh yes yes yes, oh no no no. This is the basic tension of the game—not a struggle *between* positive and negative forces but rather the exploration of what is negative, painful, or malicious *within* the ostensibly positive, whole, and benignant.

The no in the yes, the big in the little, the earth in the sky, the fight in the dance—these are the riddles Pastinha passed on, with a characteristic grand humility.

> Iê, God is great.
> Iê, God is great and I am little.
> All that I have, God gave me.
> All that I have, God have me.
> But in the roda de capoeira—
> Ha ha!
> I am a great little man.[19]

The roda is the circle in which such ironies can take place. The circle of candomblé dance is the space where human bodies incorporate divine energy. The roda de samba rather lifts humanity, secular energy, to a higher level. In capoeira, the roda contains bodies all too aware of their earthly nature. Capoeira is not contrary to the spiritual realm. And while my mother of saints voiced her disdain, many capoeiristas feel a profound link to the orixá principles, and particularly to the idea of ancestor spirits. But capoeira developed as a way of dealing with very immediate, material historical and political pressures. If the roda is viewed as a cosmographic emblem, a little map of the world of hard knocks, within that sign the capoeirista acknowledges his potential for action.

When capoeiristas pause in a game to pace—always counterclockwise—around the inner limits of the roda, this is called taking a walk around the world. But the circle is not the only sign in capoeira readable as earth. Robert Farris Thompson has analyzed in detail and with grace the variety of Kongo-derived cosmograms in the New World.[20] I have mentioned and will repeat here that the emblem of Bimba's capoeira school, while it may appear to be a mixture of Judeo-Christian and military emblems, is in fact part of the Kongo inscriptive tradition in Brazil known as *pontos riscados*.

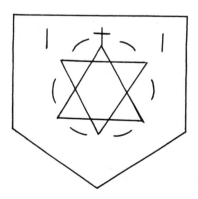

SAMBA

There is a circle, but there is also a cross—which in this context must be recognized as a crucifix, but also as a cosmological sign of the Kongo tradition. Thompson cites Wyatt MacGaffey on the Kongo sign of the cross:

> One line represents the boundary; the other is ambiva-
> lently both the path leading across the boundary, as to
> the cemetery; *and* the vertical path of power linking
> "the above" with "the below." This relationship, in turn,
> is polyvalent, since it refers to God and man, God and
> the dead, and the living and the dead.[21]

And while Bimba's school may be read by some angoleiros as having broken the roda, the protective circle of African consciousness in capoeira, its emblem rather shows a circle *made up* of discontinuity. And precisely when it would seem that Western influence— the crucifix—interrupts the circle, this sign of the cross may rather be a mark of continuity with African strategies of defense.

The sign of the cross is sometimes embodied in the players. Before entering the game, capoeiristas generally squat before the berimbau and cross them- selves—but they also touch the ground, indicating the probability of a Kongo, not just a Christian, reference. And at a certain point in an angola game, one player may pause and extend his arms, seemingly creating the sign of Christ's body. His head hangs slightly, his hands appear limp, and the gesture is one of not only apparent vulnerability but also of submission. But this gesture is in fact a challenge. The other player will demonstrate, at a distance, his wiliest moves, then ap- proach him who called the challenge. What follows may seem to a spectator to be a strange, subtle dance of exquisite gentleness, two men delicately pressing their heads to each other's shoulder, arm draped sensitively over arm, thigh just barely pressed against thigh. And then the second man, the challenged one, will spring his malice, and most likely will be surprised back with kick or sweep. This is treachery, but it doesn't mean the sensitive dance was false. All gestures of submission and openness in capoeira *can* be read as such, but they all contain the potential of violence.

The cross of the body is also set askew in the *aú*, or cartwheel, one of the most important moves of the game. The aú literally inverts the sign of the cross, demonstrating the ambivalence of "the above" and "the below" of which MacGaffey speaks.[22] In fact it sets up and down spinning. If God is in heaven, then all is right with the world. But if nothing is right in the world and hierarchies, human or divine, are set off balance, then men will invert themselves until they can make sense of it all. The cross, of course, is not only significant in Christian and Kongo symbology. It is also the sign of the crossroads, playground of Exú, a Yoruba figure. The crossroads marks the place where everything becomes relative—including good and bad. It is appropriate that it should also mark the collision of belief systems of the cultures which African Brazil comprises.

In a world of ironic inversions, which way is up? Perhaps the most beautiful *ladainha*, or extended, plaintive solo lyric of capoeira, was sung by Mestre Pastinha:

SAMBA

Already I'm fed up
of life here on the earth.
Oh mama, I'm going to the moon,
I talked to my wife about it.
She answered me,
we'll go if God wills it.
We'll make a little ranch there,
all full of greens.
Tomorrow at seven o'clock,
we'll have our breakfast.
I really can't abide
people who tell unbelievable stories.
Eh, the moon comes to the earth.
Eh, the earth goes to the moon.
All this is just talk,
now let's get to work. . . .[23]

Upside down, the sky is the ground beneath your feet, and the only heaven is the earth to which you are bound. It's an unbelievable story, but true. The plaintiveness of the ladainha is that that upside-down world is a better one than this one. It is a world where there will always be food to put on the table. But the song stops itself: all this lyricism is just talk. And the call to get to "work" is a call to action—a call to begin the game, to come back *through* the game to the ground of significance, of political reality, and of the fight.

That doesn't mean the music has to stop, nor the dance. The fight is in the dance, and the music itself, even this kind of lyricism, can be a weapon, and can be pointedly, politically significant. The berimbau is a hauntingly beautiful instrument. It consists of a curved wooden bow strung with a single wire cord, and with a resonating gourd attached at the base. The gourd pressed against his belly, the player strikes the cord with a small stick while simultaneously varying the pitch by manipulating a small stone or coin near the base of the instrument. Effectively two notes are achieved, although variations in pressure allow for a much wider spectrum of sounds. The sound emitted is an eerie twang. There is something deeply sad and mysterious about berimbau music. It is said to be an instrument of communication with the dead. There are various rhythms played for capoeira, and in this century they have been classified and categorized ad infinitum by different masters.[24] But unlike most of the highly sophisticated rhythmic patterns of African Brazil, capoeira music doesn't dictate stepping on a certain beat. Rather, the music dictates the emotional tenor of the game and its intent. The moves themselves move in and out of synchrony with the berimbau.

The rhythm isn't the only thing hard to pin down about the berimbau's sound. Pitch, too, is neither here nor there. Lewis describes this accurately:

> For some time I assumed that the interval between stopped and unstopped strings on the *berimbau* was in fact a whole tone, but upon closer listening, and comparing several bows, I realized that the interval was usually somewhat less than a whole step but more than a half-step. In Western musical terms this kind of pitch is sometimes called a "quarter tone" or (more generally) a "micro-tone," and the effect in this case is that the interval can be heard (by Western ears) either as a major second (whole step) or a minor second (half-step). In practice this means that *berimbau* music can be used to accompany songs in various modes or scales, with either a major or minor feel, but always with a slight dissonance.[25]

SAMBA

Lewis suggests that this indeterminacy might be a way of explaining the "call" of the berimbau—that quality which seems to summon a listener to participate in its musicality. As in my own earlier discussion of "bent" rhythms in the samba, the "micro-tone" explanation—enlightening as it is—is probably not quite as satisfying as the acknowledgment of axé, or spiritual energy.

A capoeira song says, "the berimbau is an instrument / that plays on just one string. / It plays angola in C-major. / But I've come to believe, old pal, / berimbau is the greatest / comrade." The simplicity of the berimbau is misleading. Pastinha said:

> A lot of people say that it's an instrument—berimbau berimbau berimbau, it's music, it's an instrument. Berimbau, then, is music, it's a musical instrument— it's also an offensive instrument. Because on the occasion of happiness, it's an instrument—we use it as an instrument. And in the hour of pain, it stops being an instrument and becomes a hand weapon.[26]

The use of the thick wooden bow as a weapon is not taught in capoeira academies. But if the wood is in hand and the occasion for violence arises, it is not difficult to imagine that uses other than musical might be made of the berimbau.

In capoeira, apparent musicality always contains violent potential, and all aggression is transformed into dance. That is why the simple opposition of categories seems to me clearly unsatisfactory. Regional and angola styles strike me rather as in dialogue with one another, and speaking, finally, the same double-talk, whether or not you call it "up-to-date." And while most scholars of the art have come down on one side of the fence (with

Lewis an exception), the majority of capoeiristas, at least until very recently, did not necessarily ally themselves with one camp—including "atual." How do you make rigid alliances in a world where you must trust everyone but can't trust anyone?

My first capoeira master in Bahia was certainly among those who refused to define his game restrictively. Mestre Boa Gente (which means "Good People") was the baddest good people I may ever have met. I wouldn't trust him as far as you could throw him, although he's weightless and wiry, so you could probably throw him pretty far if you could just get your hands on him. Mestre Boa Gente is more than just a master of capoeira. He is also a broadcaster, bar owner, local hero in the Valley of Pebbles, and a general *gato esperto:* a smart cat. Boa has one academy at the old Red Cross Club in the middle of town and another at his house in the Valley. The Vale das Pedrinhas, Valley of Pebbles, is a notorious Bahia slum. Boa Gente runs a makeshift bar there, a shack by his house where you can get a beer or a shot of rum, buy an individual cigarette, a cake of soap, chewing gum, a sanitary napkin, or a little slab of guava paste. Boa has also installed a microphone and an old turntable, and wired them up to a network of speakers throughout the Valley. The system operates at 300 watts, every day, reaching the Valley's 30,000 inhabitants. Boa plays samba and rhythm and blues, tells truths and lies about life, politics, and art.

I used to take class at the Red Cross Club, three days a week. We were a mixed lot—mixed race, mixed

SAMBA

sex, mostly domestic and service workers, myself being the only gringa. Women train increasingly in the academies, although this is really quite a recent phenomenon. While Bahia is acknowledged as the cradle of capoeira, it lags behind in drawing women into the game.[27] Academies in Rio, São Paulo and Brasília receive more women students, and capoeira classes in the United States, often held in dance studios, commonly have a fifty-fifty gender ratio. There is a female "mestra," Edna Lima, teaching out of New York. But the only women of somewhat legendary status in capoeira lore seem to be a few common-law wives of the old masters, and somebody called "Maria Doze-Homens," Twelve-Man Maria, whom nobody has ever identified for me. But Boa told me he felt women had an advantage in capoeira: in a *machista* culture, women had already been forced to learn about seduction as a weapon. Men had to study it. I learned a great deal about it myself in Brazil. If I hadn't I would have been knocked flat on my *bunda* more often even than I was. But capoeira also taught me athleticism. We trained hard in the sweltering heat, for hours at a time. Women were exempted from nothing. Sometimes, trembling through a thirtieth pushup, I'd look at Boa Gente's little sinewy body, popping up and down effortlessly as he rested just on the tips of his fingers and toes. Women have a different center of gravity, and it is difficult for many of us to remain for long upside down. Boa insisted this was no excuse—the important thing was being able to see the *world* upside down.

That means more than one thing. Certainly it means being able to see the irony in life. It also means offering another perspective on social inequity—from the underside—and in this sense women clearly have much to say in the roda. And, as Dossar has argued,[28] it means looking into that upside-down world which is the world of the dead. This last significance perhaps seems incongruous in the context of so much irony, humor, and play. But the play can be dead serious, and the world of the dead can seem altogether lively when we understand it as animated with ancestral lessons.

I used to have some friends who gave free capoeira classes to kids on evenings in a dilapidated public school in Bahia. They would often ask guest speakers to come in and tell the kids about the history of Africans in Brazil. One night at the end of class the wife of one of the teachers came in to talk about the quilombos and capoeira's historical association with black resistance. We were seated in a circle, sweaty from our workout, listening intently to this eloquent, dignified woman. She had traveled to Nigeria as an emissary from one of the carnaval groups, and on this evening she was wearing an elaborate head-tie she'd received there. As the usually wriggly kids sat somber and rapt, one by one the little wooden blocks that made up the floor began to—pop. When the first one went, several kids jumped. There was a pause, and then—pop—pop— pop. The place was going off like popcorn. A bunch of us scrambled toward the door, thinking the building was collapsing; others were too surprised to move. Once we managed to scoot everybody out into the courtyard, the popping subsided.

Afterward, the speaker's husband, who was a geologist, told the class it had been the result of an unusually rapid drop in temperature. But he told the adults in private that he had gone back to examine the structure and could find no explanation. A mãe de santo was called in, who winced and shook her head as soon as she got a whiff of all the riled-up ancestor spirits in that room. It took a heavy herb bath to get things calmed down. Apparently a righteous woman's words and all those trembling, eager, hot, hungry, muscled little bodies was too potent a combination.

But the dead can communicate as much calm and restraint as impatience and explosivity. If it is the act of physical inversion that brings one closest to the other side, then it is true that it is the angoleiro who is in closest contact with his ancestors. Angola play is deliberate, earthbound—and often inverted. Some upside-down moves occur in regional play as well, but the pace of the game usually demands that you right yourself as quickly as possible. The aú, for example, is only occasionally prolonged for effect, but is more often a swift escape maneuver. It goes spinning by like a pinwheel. In angola play, the aú is slow, meaningful, and *fechado*: "closed." It's crooked, contracted, pretzeled in on itself, knees bent, feet flexed. Unlike the Olympic-style, perfectly symmetrical cartwheel of capoeira regional, the angoleiro's aú fechado is gorgeously ugly, elegantly awkward. Closing the body means leaving it in a position of readiness and protection.

As I noted, in the candomblé, one refers to a ritually protected initiate as having a *corpo fechado*—a closed body. The trace of this operation is a raised scar on the shoulder. I have already discussed the way in which the healing of a ritual wound marks a doubled closure: of the individual into her body and into her community.[29] In the same way, the angoleiro who closes his body in the aú fechado appears to make himself vulnerable by pulling the rug out from under himself, and yet the subsequent contraction heals him not only of his vulnerability to attack but also *into* the body of racial memory and the world of his ancestors.

I rarely went on my free days to train at my master's second academy, in the Valley of Pebbles. But one night I went there with Jorge, one of Boa's older students. He was a certain type of capoeirista ("atual" doesn't do his style justice): graceful, deliberate, taciturn. He used to do a slow-motion cartwheel, bending his arms as he went over so that his head rested for an instant, delicately, on the ground. It was heart-breaking.

The night we went to the Valley, there was a strange electric crackling in the air, and little colored paper flags and Christmas-tree lights were strung up around the crossroads. The Valley is one of those unsettling, magical places in the world where you can't quite tell if the atmosphere is carnivalesque or under siege. It's both. It's dark, and firecrackers explode sporadically. Unkempt children play in little clumps in the streets. Skinny women with plucked eyebrows, ratty, straightened hair, and torn cotton dresses stand in the shadows with their arms crossed. One man goes running by, scared; another leans against a pole and pees. And over this dim scenario blasts the ecstatic, scratchy, reassuring voice of Boa Gente. He was in the studio when we arrived. Boa greeted us, cut off the record he was playing and announced that coming up was an exclusive interview with me, Barbara Browning, a

SAMBA

famous journalist from the famous American magazine-newspaper "The New York Time." I'm neither famous nor a journalist, connected to neither *Time* nor the *Times*, but Boa can't resist a good interview. Jorge, "Dr. Jorge," he claimed, was a famous dentist who would come back later to give the people of the Valley some tips on oral hygiene. Jorge, who worked in fact as a "boy" in an office building, looked mortified. Lucky for him, he never had to give his interview on oral hygiene. But I did get a good on-air grilling on poverty and multinational corporate politics. Finally Boa pointed at the somber little gang of skinny kids clustered around the studio door. He asked me if, as a famous journalist, I felt that the American public heard enough about hungry Brazilian children. Sweating, I answered quite solemnly that, as a famous journalist, I felt Americans didn't hear enough about that. Boa put a record on, and gave me a hug and a drink.

Boa Gente tells truths and lies. I'd like to say that I believe that he does not suffer from lapses of honesty. Rather, these small falsehoods are a demonstration of the *rigor* which Boa exercises in regard to truth. When I met him, I thought I had encountered the incarnation of a Nietzschean principle. Nietzsche wrote that the truth needs to confront opposition from time to time and be able to fight. We need to pit truth against falsehood or it will grow tiresome, powerless, and insipid—and we with it. This is Boa's game. I gave him a Portuguese translation of *Beyond Good and Evil* for his birthday, and inscribed it:

> To Master Boa Gente, who taught me
> that beauty can be a weapon, and
> strength can be an art.

How could you classify capoeira as a dance or a fight? One seldom strikes a blow to hit—more often to demonstrate the beauty of the movement, and to harmonize it with the movements of the other. And the most powerful players are those who incapacitate their opponents by doing some stunning trick of pure gorgeousness: a flip, a slow, twisting cartwheel, a head-spin, or just a graceful *ginga*, the swaying dance step that comes between blows. A capoeirista can have such a pretty ginga, arms twisting in impossible beautiful waves, that it *confuses*.

It was my first master who taught me the philo-sophical implications of the beauty and illusion of capoeira. That's why I came to syncretize, in my mind, Boa Gente with Nietzsche—and, of course, Exú. In the Catholic context, Exú has defied syncretism. His pairing with the devil is misleading. Exú is more playful than evil. Jorge Amado says he is "just a deity in constant motion, friend of fracas, of confusion; but, in his heart of hearts, an excellent person. In a way he is the No where only Yes exists."[30]

Exú, Boa, Friedrich: they make up a trinity. They are the No in the Yes, the Falsehood in Truth, the big mixup, the good laugh. It's an inverted trinity, just as the sign of the cross is inverted in the roda.

Many of capoeira's maneuvers are inversions, whether literal or ironic, physical or linguistic. One of the most basic blows is called the bênção (blessing or benediction).[31] But instead of giving a good word or ex-tending a pious hand, the capoeirista "blesses" with the sole of his foot, shooting it forward toward the other player's chest. The move is at least physically perfectly straightforward. But the response to it is usually an exaggerated pantomime of getting clobbered: part of the defense actually might be to fake getting hit, although that rarely happens. The one receiving the blow may even issue an ear-piercing shriek, snapping back his head in mock deflection of the kick. Sometimes this kind of defense is more dramatic, more satisfying than the blow itself.

Capoeira defensive moves are not so much blocks or even counterattacks as they are ironic negations of the offense.[32] The basic defensive position is called, in fact, the *negativa*. The player squats, one crooked leg extended, and leans forward and across this leg, pressing the side of his head toward the ground. To the uninitiated, it feels like an almost impossibly uncomfortable, impractical, and vulnerable position. But it is the ground zero from which a vast number of deep maneuvers can be deployed.

The low-to-the-ground moves are the ones most often used in capoeira angola. They don't look efficient—who would think to bend over and look through his legs in order to fight? But they are wily and sly. Many moves are named after animals, such as the stingray-tail, an unexpected backlash, or the monkey, a lopsided back flip. The apparent impracticality of these acts has to be understood within the context of creating irony. To regard the animal references as evidence of the "natural" origins of capoeira seems to me a limited idea. Rather, these references seem to be in part ironic responses to projections on black culture in Brazil of stereotypes of innocence. A 1980 ethnography[33] cited an Angolan informant who suggested that capoeira had developed from an ancient Angolan ritual called "the dance of the zebra," in which young men imitated a mating ritual of zebras, fighting to win first choice of the young marriageable women. This document was quickly absorbed by some members of the capoeira angola contingent who began circulating the story. It is not unreasonable to suggest that some of the maneuvers of capoeira were inspired by animal motion. But I have also heard of a dubious older angoleiro who, on hearing this story, shook his head: "The only 'dance of the zebra' I ever saw was in the zoo, and it was two zebras fucking."

That kind of cynicism isn't a self-wounding rejection of Africa. And maybe a romanticized version of Africa has to exist on a certain level in capoeira history. But when it is ridiculed, it is also an affirmation of the developments of black culture in urban Brazil. Regional moves are self-ironizing as well. Bimba himself had a trick of "modernizing" capoeira while simultaneously making fun of modern technologies and of Western influences. He developed a sock to the head which set the ears ringing and called it the "telefone." That joke strikes me as remarkably reminiscent of the Nigerian "naive" (ironic!) novelist Amos Tutuola who introduces a character with a "voice like a telephone" in the middle of the wildest, deepest, most "African" bush, residence of ancestral spirits.[34] Another of Bimba's head-banging techniques was a knockout punch called "godême," his phonetic transcription of the "God damn it" gasped by a U.S. marine who got busted in his challenge to the master. If people complained he was incorporating boxing techniques, he Brazilianized those blows and made them capoeira.

SAMBA

A friend sighed to me recently, watching a rapid-fire, exquisitely executed regional game, "capoeira has really developed into a sophisticated art over the last twenty years." It's true that some regionalistas are remarkable athletes. Their speed, flexibility, precision, and strength seem in perfect harmony. But for all that I will defend the validity of their modifications on the game— they continue cannibalizing gymnastics, kick-boxing, ballet, and, in the '80s, break dancing (a form that some have speculated was at least partly derived from or inspired by capoeira)[35]—it is still an old-fashioned, flat-footed, earthbound game of angola that brings tears to my eyes. Capoeira angola's wit is defter and more stunning than any feat of athleticism. I'm certainly not alone. Perhaps the most sought-after master in New York today is João Grande—Big John—an old-guard angoleiro of Bahia, former student of Pastinha.

It isn't just a question of wit. Nor is it just that an angoleiro's play is funky with wisdom that's been fermenting for centuries. Young, politicized angoleiros have a point. It is important to reaffirm—constantly— the history of capoeira as an art of resistance. Hot dog regionalistas can spin so fast they sometimes lose sight of the past, and the present. The postmodern cultural critic must acknowledge that she, too, is a product of the times. We're sometimes giddy with the new language available to us for expressing our enthusiasms for cultural cross-fertilization. But in rejecting a restrictive, static notion of cultural authenticity, we risk losing some of the political potential of rootedness, of respect for deep funk, of the eloquence of an old man's body in motion.

Beyond the issue of tradition and modification, capoeira also raises the more general problem of "playing" politics. The black consciousness movement in Brazil has been hampered by conflicting strategies. But both traditionalist and syncretic enclaves might appear, to North American eyes, to fall prey to an overly aestheticized idea of activism. It's true of the class struggle as well. Every political rally in Brazil degenerates (explodes?) into music minutes after its inception. Everybody is in motion—but is it progressive motion or simply a circular dance which expends energy without changing the world? That's the familiar question asked of carnaval.[36] To an outsider, capoeira may appear particularly ineffective as a martial art, since so much of its energy is expended on dance—on motion for the sake of pleasure.

But the capoeiristas say that in life, as in capoeira, you have to keep doing the ginga, dancing between the blows. Maybe it's true. The political and economic situation in Brazil has been so bad for so long, sometimes it seems inevitable that these people will get disheartened. What hope would be left if there weren't that distant, exciting rumble of the samba and the scratchy voice of Boa Gente on the air? I wish, in fact, his voice could carry across the water and make us feel watched over here in New York. I miss Loremil terribly. I feel like when he went sky-rocketing out of here, he burst a hole in the electrified firmament. It's 3 A.M. in another city that is part war zone, part ecstatic celebration.

SAMBA

I imagine Boa Gente could be on the air now, live from the Valley of Pebbles. And he could be saying the words of Nietzsche's Zarathustra:

> Lift up your hearts, my brethren, high, higher! And do not forget your legs! Lift up also your legs, ye good dancers—and better still if ye stand also on your heads!

4. **Of the Daughters of Gandhi and the Dance of the Chicken**

Friday is the day of Oxalá, Big Daddy in the Sky, and on this Friday that opens the carnaval of Bahia my sister *sócias* of the carnaval group the Daughters of Gandhi and I convene in the old part of the city to offer Him libations and ask for peaceful festivities. The oldest Daughters sing and we clap and respond, then our chests are splashed with a cool, gritty mixture of cornmeal and water which will leave us smelling sweet like corn all that afternoon and evening, despite the oppressive heat.

SAMBA

We are a mild-mannered afoxé, distinct from the showy *blocos*. The *blocos afro*, African blocs, are the most spectacular aspect of the Bahian carnaval, some comprising thousands of members, with massive, complex, and perfectly rehearsed drum corps. The afoxés are generally more modest and are linked to houses of candomblé. Ours is a little band, the only all-women group. Our rhythm section is made up of adolescent boys who couldn't make the grade for our fabulously famous brother organization, the Sons of Gandhi. The Sons of Gandhi, founded in 1949, are among the most respected of Bahian institutions, known for their maturity, elegance, and pacifism (a reputation only slightly marred by local political clientelism). When the Sons parade en masse, the street becomes a sea of white robes and turbans, slashed by royal blue ribbons and beads. Our group is a mere puddle of similar garments, feminized. We are a sentimental favorite, but few choose to march with us. Not a lot of women want to spend carnaval segregated from the men. All the blocos are mixed sex. But I always accompany the Daughters. Many of our members are very old women. I like to watch them dance to conserve energy. It's a different groove from the frenetic youth crews. And there's another advantage: the Sons are always somewhere nearby, and they look out for us.

The headquarters of our organization is together with theirs, in Pelourinho, the old city. When I went there for the first time to inscribe myself as a Daughter, I was attended at the desk by a small elderly man in a jacket and bow tie—a peculiar outfit for a fellow on a stifling, unairconditioned Bahian summer afternoon. He sat me down and asked some questions in a florid, formal fashion. He told me I couldn't be attended yet by the women's representative, but I should wait. He talked. A lot. I waited. The woman I needed to see, it was finally determined, would only be in the following afternoon. I was told to come back. I went back the next day, not to find my inscriber but to find the little man well prepared and waiting for me. He had a carefully typed though slightly yellowed poem, with an inscription handwritten to me. The typing said:

FASCINATION . . .
A Love Poem

Written by: Ajurymar de Sant'Anna

Hear me
And with your beautiful eyes that God
Gave you, read my verses.
Caress me with your thoughts
While sleep watches over my body.
Kiss me with your dainty hands
Because my lips will reciprocate.
Speak to me like a child for the ears of my life
Will open like flowers
In the moist and infinite dawn.

Ajurymar handed me the poem only after reciting it in hushed reverence and ceremoniously kissing my hand. But the representative would not be in until the next day.

The next day I returned to find Ajurymar passionately reciting to another young prospective Daughter: " . . . with your dainty hands, because my lips will reciprocate . . ." She had a blank, overheated expression, as though she'd been sitting there for a while. Still, no representative. Our group pulled its act together at the last minute. Membership receipts were stamped and signed by a sweaty eight-month pregnant woman, the line snaking through a crumbling building with a lot of dangling electric cables. Around us, other Daughters were fitting costumes, sewing on extra sequined appliqués, admiring the simple white sandals, complaining about the lack of organization, reminiscing about the previous year's carnaval.

The Daughters of Gandhi (recently redesignated "Daughters of Oxum"), during our scheduled processions, do not exhibit elaborate choreographies. We wade through the packed streets, cordoned off by guards, marking Yemanjá's simple steps with the restraint of initiates who have seen all this before. We do not dance topless, or invent new moves. Our rhythm, like that of all such groups, is also popularly called afoxé, but its technical name is *ijexá*. It is a secularized version of the rhythm played for Oxum in the candomblé, and perhaps that is why we maintain a certain decorum.

But those of us under, say, fifty, those of us still prone to dizziness at the sight of a hundred pairs of youthful muscled arms pounding music together out of a hundred skins—we also go to see the modern blocos—Olodum, Ara Kêtu, Muzenza, or perhaps the most glorious, Ilê Aiyê. It isn't enough to see them arrive in the square at the center of town. The real party, the place where something really happens, is at the several headquarters, invariably in the poorest areas of town: Pelourinho, Liberdade, Perí-Perí. . . . The neighborhood comes out to send its home bloco off, and on his own turf each drummer is a local hero. Each neighborhood, each bloco, has established its own particular rhythm, which is specified by name. To foreign ears, they may be difficult to distinguish, as they are all thunderous variations on the samba. But devotees can develop strong preferences, and the men who create the beat are articulating local pride. The drummers are not the only stars. These blocos also have dance soloists aboard truck platforms, executing gorgeously athleticized versions of orixá choreographies. And on the ground, the real heros of the bloco, its members at large, forge new popular steps out of religious, secular, foreign, and homegrown moves.

The blocos afro grew throughout the 1980s, rapidly becoming the cornerstone of the Bahian carnaval. While Rio begawds itself for the onslaught of tourists and pulses to an ecstatic samba rhythm, the Bahian carnaval has remained stubbornly popular. And while it is certainly spectacular, it is an earthy, neighborhoody affair.

Prior to the surge of the blocos, the Bahian carnaval was a ragtag mix of several forms: the afoxés; the *blocos de índio*, Indian-identified, hard-drinking samba crews; and the impossibly irritating and yet sort of lovable *trios elétricos*, hyperamplified, super-high-speed hokey pop ensembles aboard huge floats, followed by masses of pom-pom-shaking, crazed youths of various races (though, clearly, the trios attracted a lighter-skinned following than the afro- or índio-identified groups). These styles clashed surprisingly happily in the streets for five days, each group not merely putting up with but actually grooving on each other's rhythm. But with the merging of samba with afoxé and other rhythms, the blocos afro developed a sound that soon eclipsed the trios' "frero" rhythm. Today, even the trios play electrified versions of bloco afro carnaval hits. And in turn, the blocos are increasingly adding an electric, harmonic element to their percussion ensembles.

Probably the best-known and most influential rhythm of the modern blocos afros is called samba-reggae. It was developed and popularized by the musical director of the bloco Olodum, Neguinho (Little Black Guy) do Samba. The two poles of influence are apparent in the name of the rhythm. It is a relatively small minority of Bahians who are particularly well versed in Rastafarian doctrine, and probably fewer still who are aware of some of the connections between their own and the Jamaicans' syncretic, resistant beliefs. But the people understand the *beat* of reggae as signifi-cant of black consciousness, and this significance lends a certain gravity to the samba. The cross-fertilization of these rhythms has engendered a new music of unde-niable force.

Samba-reggae is heavy on the *surdo*, the deafen-ing bass drum. Unlike Rio-style samba, the multiple surdos of the blocos alternate in complicated, fre-quently broken phrases. The different tuning of the drums gives the percussion a developed melodic feel, with another heavily broken stick line on top.

The layering of samba and reggae rhythms may sound at first like an incongruity. Reggae, everybody knows, is heavy, funky, and deep. Samba has depth to familiar ears, but it gives an initial impression of light-speed and a mercurial ability to bead up and skim the rhythmic surface. And yet when reggae and samba come together they seem to draw out each other's submerged qualities. It was a *shekere* player who first drew my attention to the fact that reggae is a 6/8 rhythm. Shekere, the lopped-off gourd strung with an external net of beads, is an instrument that slips beautifully into the pocket of a 6/8. My friend said, "Watch this." He played a simple 6/8 and on the fourth and sixth eight-note he chuk-ha'd the strum of a reggae pickup. That 6/8 is the same double triplet that underlies the samba—another apparently squared rhythm. In the samba, that rolling undercurrent is layed over with rapid-fire top patterns. In reggae, the bass obscures it. But together the light and dark illuminate each other. Samba-reggae is profoundly funky, but breaks over the top even more brilliantly than Rio samba.

It is possible to dance samba-reggae as a samba, and the devout do. But the Bahian homeboys take it in a dance-hall stylee. And everything in between is also possible. The biggest popular step yet developed for the rhythm is a *dança da galinha*, the dance of the chicken. It doesn't sound very elegant, and it isn't, unless you have a particularly Bahian sense of elegance. Stepping simply right-left-right-left on the basic four beats of the squared phrase, you waddle forward, or possibly backward, in little shifting steps, wagging your behind from side to side. It looks more like a duck, truth be told, than a chicken. Meanwhile your arms flap before you or, in retro, behind you. There have subsequently developed variations on this theme: arms flapping to one side or another, ankles twisting in an extra little flick, a double behind-wag. . . . The dance of the chicken recalls one of capoeira's etymologies—the

SAMBA

chicken coop—and it seems to play on that same stereotype of frenzied, uncontrolled motion. But the dance is deceptively difficult, the subtleties of ankle-flicking hard to describe. It requires a certain sense of *suingue*, as Bahians say, or swing.

Out of this came other dances: the *dança do tortinho*, the dance of the crooked little guy, an extra-mangled version that has a special contorted charm; the *dança do ti ti ti*, an aggressively hyperactive scooting from side to side with the arms extended, flailing, overhead; and the *dança do crocodilo*, where an entire trio elétrico dance crew forms itself into a kind of undulating crocodile tail, something like the "wave" of football stadiums in the United States.

Several years ago, carnaval dance style took a new turn with the advent of the *deboche*. *Deboche* is debauchery, and the dance brought the principle down to a verb: debochar. A carnaval pop star named Luis Caldas began promoting a syrupy pop sound that mixed the blocos' funk with the trio's frenzy. The dance it provoked can only be described as extreme sensual celebration: looser than the dance of the chicken, the deboche allows every part of the body free play. Deboche has been as contagious as the fictional epidemic funk "Jes Grew" of Ishmael Reed's *Mumbo Jumbo*. Even with the gravely political lyrics of their songs blasting out over the blocos afro, the bodies on the street drip with this sweetness.

Finally, a word must be said about the lambada. I first heard the word used in the early '80s in Bahia. But the style of dance, I was told even then, had been popular for years in the northeast. Essentially, the lambada is like a two-step merengue. There is nothing particularly fancy about it. It's true that Bahians tend to take the idea of hip-to-hip to the letter, but the cinematic export versions involving S and M back-snapping dips didn't develop in Brazil. Two clever Frenchmen took the dance to Paris, where it came to signify a kind of mythic sexual abandon that has always been part of the French conception of Brazil. Famous, lambada went back to Brazil quite transformed, and it burned out from hype almost as fast on its home turf as it did in the United States. For a time, every health club in Rio and São Paulo had classes, with unsuspecting women in funny skirts getting slammed for the dip. That's not to say there's no charm in dancing lambada—it *is* sensual. At this point it's difficult to separate the *physical* sensuality from the ideas of eroticism which have been grafted onto the dance. My young friends would joke, seeing a pregnant girl, that she'd "gotten a lambada." The name itself has strange resonances. *Lamber* means to lick, but it also means a licking in the sense of a beating. This is an odd, hybrid dance which combined internal and external stereotypes of Brazilian sexuality. It dominated the musical scene briefly. But the carnaval wasn't made for couples' dances. It demands freedom of movement: deboche, galinha.

When I say that there are both internal and external stereotypes of Brazilian sexuality which get played out in dance, I should add that these stereotypes are sometimes difficult to distinguish and always difficult to disentangle from one another. As Richard Parker has observed,

> Brazilians view themselves as sensual beings not
> simply in terms of their individuality . . . but at
> a social or cultural level—as sensual individuals,

at least in part, by virtue of their shared *brasilidade*,
or "Brazilianness."[1]

All myths erase their points of origin, but the trail of the
development of a myth of Brazilian sensuality is not
hard to trace. I've already covered part of the ground
in my discussion of sexuality and miscegenation in
Brazilian social theory.[2] But even prior to the crucible of
racial mixing—in fact, at the first moment of European
contact with Brazil—there was already a complex of
figures for Brazil as an erotic paradise.[3]

Pêro Vaz de Caminha, a clerk who accompanied
the first colonial expedition to Brazil, wrote a letter
describing the indigenous women he encountered
on his arrival. This letter contains a joke which turns
on a sixteenth-century Portuguese euphemism for a
woman's genitalia: *vergonha*, or "shame":

> among them were three or four young very nice young
> ladies with long black hair hanging down their backs,
> and with their "shames" so high and tight and clean of
> hair that we were able to look at them without any
> shame whatsoever.[4]

There is no shame in looking, or in showing. And Pêro
Vaz even goes on to say that it's a shame that Portuguese ladies don't have "shames" comparable to
those which the Brazilians have, and yet *of* which they
have none.

Nakedness only becomes exhibitionism when it
is reflected back through another's shame. But one
wouldn't want to repeat the reduction of Brazilian
social practice to a bad Portuguese joke. The Brazilians
had their own cultural proscriptions prior to the arrival
of Pêro Vaz—and, in all likelihood, they had their own

shame. Contemporary Brazilians are by no means unself-conscious about their sexuality, nor about their perceived "shamelessness." If anything, they have a doubled self-reflexivity.

While variations of "sensual" dances such as the deboche and the dance of the chicken proliferate, samba-reggae also accommodates a range of steps that used to be the domain of the afoxés. These moves are secularized candomblé dances, and are heavily significant. As I have written, candomblé is an extension of mostly Yoruba beliefs, but the blocos afro are dedicated to celebrating the cultures of all African nations. Each year, each bloco celebrates a particular culture in the carnaval. A group may sing songs in praise of Senegal, for example, mentioning great figures in Senegalese history, but they may in the same breath invoke the orixás of candomblé. This is by no means a question of misinformation. The carnaval composers research carefully the distinctive cultures of which they write. But for black Bahians, the Yoruba orixás signify a commitment to their Africanness generally. At the same time, they incorporate African diasporic rhythms—reggae, mambo, merengue—into their own music, acknowledging its complex origins and articulating it all through the samba. It sounds terribly complicated, and it is, but the brilliance is in balancing African nationalism with attention to cultural specificity—one's own and others'.

Not all critics have perceived this process as fruitful. In the only published English-language study of the Bahian carnaval, *African Myth and Black Reality in Bahian Carnival*, Daniel Crowley laments the "naive

pan-africanism" of both the afoxés and the blocos afro.[5]
By leaping arbitrarily between African and diasporic
cultures, Crowley asserts, the blocos lose sight of certain historical and political realities. Christopher Dunn,
however, has challenged Crowley's critique:

> At one level one might ask, what is the "real" African
> past? . . . To some extent, all histories must rely on
> mythic prefigurations in order to render the past
> meaningful and coherent. In this sense, the *afoxés* and
> *blocos afro* are not so much spreading misinformation
> about Africa, as constructing a powerful, grass-roots
> discourse which challenges traditional notions and
> myths of Africans and their descendants in Brazil.[6]

While the bloco afro composers avail themselves of the
published histories and ethnographies of African states
and cultures, they are aware of the woeful inadequacy
of many of these accounts. Their very notion of history
defies the capacity of the West to inscribe Africanness.

Western historiographers are increasingly sensitive
to this kind of critique. As Steven Feierman has written,

> Historians now understand the dubious criteria
> according to which women and Africans, peasants
> and slaves were excluded from the histories of earlier
> generations. . . . The previously excluded histories do
> not only present new data to be integrated into the
> larger narrative; they raise questions about the validity
> of that narrative itself.[7]

A linear account of cultures which assumes the univer-
sality of the privileging of linearity is off to a false start.
The Bahian carnaval rewrites African history in terms
which are meaningful to its participants. This inscription
includes the orixás, even in accounts of non-Yoruba

cultures. Much of the West's confusion regarding the Afro-Brazilian worldview generally seems to stem from an inability—or refusal—to take seriously the orixás as legitimate principles which can cross cultures.

Beyond retelling history, the blocos are educating the Bahian public about contemporary political issues, at home and abroad. Their interest in the political struggles of African states is, again, not a "naive pan-africanism" but a reasoned recognition that, as largely underclass Brazilians, the members share many difficulties (individual and communal) with their African brothers and sisters. This affiliation is not simply racial. Perhaps the instance which illustrated this most clearly was Olodum's choice, in 1990, to celebrate not an African nation but the northeastern region of Brazil itself. The *nordeste* is understood as delimiting not merely a geographic terrain but a terrain of character as well. The very name of the area evokes images of agricultural and human devastation. The northeast is regularly racked by drought. It has by far the lowest per capita income and highest mortality rate in the country. Although technically the entire state of Bahia is included in the region, the word nordeste is usually used to signify the interior of the region—seemingly a world apart from the lush, coastal city of Salvador. There is another difference. Although the nordeste is also known for racial mixing, the predominant component is indigenous, not African.

Despite its wasted, humiliated face in the Brazilian imagination, the nordeste is the site of legendary moments of resistance. In its 1990 carnaval lyrics, Olodum celebrated several of them. A nineteenth-century Christian mystic, Antonio Conselheiro, apparently under divine inspiration, led a peasant revolt which culminated in the death of virtually all of his followers.[8] He is remembered today less for his anointment by God than for refusing to put up with any more shit, regardless of the cost. Lampião and Maria Bonita were something like the backlands' Bonnie and Clyde—fearless looters who eluded the authorities for years. And Zumbi was an escaped slave who ruled over the most famous of the quilombos, Palmares. Zumbi was African—but none of the other figures were, and they were all lumped together in Olodum's celebration not because of race but because they signify a history of oppositional politics in Brazil. Race *is* an element of this story, but identification is made across racial boundaries.

When I first "went out" with the Daughters of Gandhi, I was probably the lightest-skinned woman in the lot, or would have been without a rigorous precarnaval beach schedule. (I also had my hair "Africanized"—braided into thread-fine braids, twisted into a complex configuration.) I never felt I stood out racially in my group, as we really comprised the spectrum of skin tones. But some blocos are very aware of their racial makeup. As the blocos have grown in popularity—particularly Olodum, which recorded in 1990 with Paul Simon—they have raised their membership dues and lightened their color considerably. (I would not attribute Olodum's celebration of Brazilian, not African, resistance that year to the event of this international recording. In fact, Olodum's leadership expressed dismay that neither Simon nor the international public seemed to be acknowledging the group as racially politicized.)[9] Still, there is one group that remains resolutely black—because skin color is actually stipulated by its charter. Ilê Aiyê was organized as the first exclusively black group in response to a trio carnaval society which rejected persons who were "too" black. That group, the Internacionáis, soon revoked its policy. But the year that Ilê Aiyê made its triumphant counterresponse to racism, flooding the streets of Bahia with elegantly African-robed deep black women and men proclaiming their racial pride, nobody could say it wasn't a gorgeous sight to see. A decade later, you still have to have mahogany skin and "crisp" hair to join. Some other blocos call this racism. But *still* nobody can say Ilê Aiyê isn't gorgeous. And its carnaval processions have never been marked by racial violence or even disharmony.

Members of Ilé Aiyê always cite the exclusive policy of the Internacionáis as the reason for the group's founding. But it also happened to coincide with the independence of Portugal's former colonies in Africa: Angola, Mozambique, Cape Verde, Guinea-Bisau, São Tomé and Principe. The year was 1974. The map of the world was getting revised. But the group whose racism brought about Ilê continued—and continues—to cling to the old, colonial map. The Internacionáis take their name from the group's "commemoration" each year of a different nationality. But their "Chinese" or "Arabian" themes are an entirely different phenomenon from the blocos' celebration of African nations. Sometimes the Internacionáis choose make-believe

characters instead. Their "China" is as fantastic as the fictional worlds they represent. Their mascot is a pirate,
and this is one of the fantasy themes that has been used
repeatedly. Their attitude toward world cultures seems
to be something like "pillage and caricature."

It is of vital importance that the carnaval be ever
fresh, that the rhythms revise and renew themselves,
so by the time this book goes to press there will probably be a new turn of events. But for the carnaval
seasons of 1993 and 1994, the turn was Timbalada. The
percussionist and composer Carlinhos Brown founded
the group for the saint's day street party season in
1990, and it first hit the carnaval in 1992. In the next
two years, the group exploded. Timbalada is named for
the instrument played by practically everybody in the
percussion ensemble. The *timbau* is a lightweight
standing drum, similar in form to the atabaques of the
candomblé but much easier to carry and play. Timbalada is neither an afoxé, a bloco, nor a trio. There is no
name for its characteristic rhythm, a mixture of Afro-
Brazilian, African American, and Afro-Caribbean beats.
But Timbalada is less explicitly Afrocentric than the
blocos and afoxés. One member suggested to me that
the group expresses the aesthetic of *a raça baiana*: the
Bahian race. The group's regionalism would appear to
distance it from either a mythic or a "real" Africa, and
even from other black cultural groups in other parts of
Brazil. But the vast majority of Bahians—and practically
all the members of Timbalada—have dark skin.

If the group doesn't say this, they effectively show
it, and the contrast is all the starker since they began
painting their bodies. Reminiscent of the famous Keith

Haring painting on Bill T. Jones's graphic black body, Timbalada members go out covered with stark white designs. They create an astonishing image. They claim this idea was more cost-effective than making elaborate costumes the way the blocos afro do. But the body painting can be read in a number of other ways. As I've said, it demands, first of all, that you read the ground of the writing as black skin. It also seems to play on stereotypes of "savage" self-decoration in Brazil. Indigenous Brazilians continue to use body paint, and in the candomblé houses, women and men are also painted on the occasion of their initiation. Another association might well be that of the *caras pintadas*, the "painted faces": these were the young students and professionals who took to the streets in protest of the previous administration's corruption, effectively provoking President Fernando Collor's downfall in 1992. These students were mostly white or light-skinned, and they smeared their faces with grease paint—often in the colors of the Brazilian flag—to demonstrate themselves as signifying Brazil's uncorrupt future. Of course, if Brazil's intellectuals truly are to cast off inequity and corruption, they will have to see to it that race-based educational disparity ends. There should have been more black caras pintadas.

But the members of Timbalada to whom I have talked have made no connection between their own painted faces and those of the caras pintadas. In fact, when I suggested it, they denied it quite vehemently. And this is perhaps part of the last significance of this body painting which I will offer: the designs are abstract, not representational. They don't refer specifically

SAMBA

to the candomblé, nor to the Tupi-Guaraní, nor to Bill T. Jones, nor to the caras pintadas. They demand a suspended signification which allows for a less restrictive identification. It is a racial identification, but not a reductive negritude. It is a national identification, but not according to the categories of Brazilian authority and opposition delimited by whites.

Much has been said regarding the "pressure-valve" theory of Brazilian carnaval.[10] The concern is that the carnaval functions as an all-too-efficient manner of letting off the steam of social frustrations that might otherwise be directed toward political change. Moviegoers in the United States and Europe were fascinated by the poetic representation of this irony in *Black Orpheus (Orfeu Negro*, Marcel Camus, 1958). Making the candomblé more accessible to international audiences by doubling it with Greek mythology, the film demonstrated the tragedy of a fictional carnaval world of beauty and wealth which could not translate into literal, material betterment for the Brazilian people. Vinícius de Moraes's melancholy lyric for the popular song from the film went:

> Sadness has no end.
> Happiness does. . . .
> The happiness of the poor man seems
> to be the grand illusion of carnaval.
> Folks work
> all year
> for one moment of a dream
> to realize the fantasy
> of a king or a pirate or gardener—
> but it all comes to an end on Ash Wednesday.

Everyone knows that in Rio impoverished women and men go hungry in order to save money for the extraordinarily lavish costumes they will parade in with their samba schools. Over the years, most of the samba schools have come under the control of the mafia of illegal numbers runners, and the carnaval has become lucrative only to them and the tourist industry.[11] The spectacle is now enclosed in the enormous "sambadrome," where only paying spectators—many of them foreigners—can observe.

It's a cynical development, and yet the poor participants continue to sing some songs of protest, trying to mark the celebration their own glorious moment. In Bahia, however, carnaval remains steadfastly in the street. And while blocos, trios, and afoxés all charge for membership, it's possible to go out on one's own, pressing in on the cordoned-off, security-guarded groups as they steamroll down the avenue. While the songs of Rio's samba schools have always retained a degree of irony and political savvy, the songs of the blocos afro are unironically, powerfully politicized. The costumes of the Rio schools recall European pageantry and luxury; the members of the blocos dress rather as African royalty, and their fantasy, while it is a fantasy, has not been marred by cynicism.

Bakhtin taught us that carnivalization is a subversive inversion of power: the poor play rich, the weak play powerful. To speak of these inversions as "play" is not to diminish their social significance. Other inversions also play themselves out. Racial inversions in Rio's carnaval are readily apparent. In Bahia, the process is more complicated. African pride is not the only game.

SAMBA

There are the old samba groups I have mentioned which are "Indian"-identified—the most popular being the Apaches and the Comanches. These groups have mostly black members. I noted earlier that samba historically has been associated with the caboclo of the candomblé, a complex figure that links blacks literally, politically, to another disempowered group. But, as I argued, the caboclo also represents figuratively the resistant black. The Apaches and the Comanches, however, are not, apparently, caboclos. These are North American "Indian" references, and they play on the images of U.S. Wild West films, known as "bang-bang" (pronounced bangy-bangy) pictures in Brazil. The costumes recall bang-bang getups.

A person from the United States can't help but connect them to the Indian organizations of the New Orleans Mardi Gras. Also a black institution, the Mardi Gras Indians combine a literal cultural and political affiliation with a metaphorical one. Members of the Mardi Gras Indian groups have asserted that there exists a genuine racial link as well. While some cultural contact and intermarriage between blacks and Native Americans in Louisiana certainly did and does take place, most students of the Mardi Gras find the association a useful construction.[12] In fact, much like the blocos de índio, the Mardi Gras Indians appear to have been modeled on the Wild West carnival shows of the late nineteenth century. The Mardi Gras Indians have developed a complex language of their own, which renders their songs nearly indecipherable to those outside the community. But they are difficult to read in another sense. As George Lipsitz has put it, the phenomenon "projects a cultural indeterminacy":[13] neither "really" Indian nor "purely" African, its complexity is the point.

The choice of a North American Indian stereotype in Brazil is more complicated still. It sets askew the process of carnivalization by putting it in an international context. If the indigenous Brazilians were colonized by the Portuguese in the sixteenth century, Brazil in the twentieth century has found itself under U.S. pressures both economic and cultural. The influence of the bang-bang is a case in point. A black Brazilian's choosing to portray himself as an Apache marks him as the conquered but dangerous other in a game involving the whites not only of his own culture but of the United States as well.

Not only the costumes recall western films. The behavior of these groups seems patterned after the lawless, hooting troublemaking of their cinematic counterparts. The Apaches are especially known for violent rampages. In the late seventies, some members of the mostly male group surprised a women's carnaval group (no longer in existence), sexually molesting dozens of them. It was a scandal that cast the "Indian" blocos in a terrible light, and the Apaches nearly went under. It is difficult to recuperate any meaning from such an episode. Dunn's assessment of the Indian blocs, in contrast to his extremely sympathetic account of the blocos afro, is that "the notoriously rowdy, and sometimes violent *blocos índio* rebelled against white Bahian society, yet failed to articulate themselves politically."[14] And Daniel Touro Linger has written generally of acts of violence during the carnaval:

> whether one discovers in Carnival political inspiration or apolitical reverie, Carnival counterposes a utopian world vision to a socially constructed, culturally imagined, and experientially insistent "real world" infused by competition, hierarchy, frustration, and violence.
>
> But ironically, within Carnival itself this real world resurges in its most concentrated form.[15]

Linger calls the apparently unfocused, explosive violence of carnaval (what is called *briga* in Portuguese) an "unnerving dance" of social unrest.

The particular form the notorious Apache attack took—sexual—makes it not only especially horrific but also especially linked to stereotypical representations of dangerous Indians. Fear of indigenous North Americans' cultural and racial difference has always been linked to a sexual threat: the defilement of white womanhood. While the women attacked were not in the majority white, they became figurally "whitened" in the event, by coming to represent the object of an Indian threat. This is a troubling suggestion, and not merely because we know that scandalously little attention is given in both the Brazilian and U.S. media to the reality of sexual violence against women of color. What is perhaps even more disturbing is that a woman raped can certainly not be accounted for as "mere" representation, and the individual responsibility for such an act cannot be elided by metaphors. But acts of violence and perhaps especially acts of sexual violence do take place in a context of racial significations. While the figure of the Indian—the Apache of U.S. cinema—is a highly fictionalized representation, the sexual attack seems in retrospect to have demonstrated the literal fallout of racist representations.

Depictions of the violence and savagery of indigenous Brazilians and North Americans, of course, didn't begin with Wild West shows and shoot-'em-up pictures. The earliest colonial documents countered all those sexy Earthly Paradise stories with grave warnings about cannibalism. In fact, cannibalism and sexuality seem inextricably linked in these accounts. Richard Parker has quite brilliantly suggested that the carnaval itself cannibalizes the social theorists' myth of miscegenation as a sexual and racial fusion, spitting it back out as a "juxtaposition of differences."[16] And he reminds us of the cannibal reference in the grounding sexual metaphor of "those who eat":

> Given all the sexual and sensual connotations of the act of eating in Brazilian culture, the symbolism of anthropophagy is especially well suited to the semantic structure of the *carnaval*. The transgression of a food taboo can easily be linked to the transgression of sexual taboos in a symbolic construct focused on devouring the flesh of another human body in order to incorporate it within one's own. As a symbol of incorporation, then, anthropophagy can be invested with layers of meaning ranging from cannibalism itself, to the act of sexual intercourse, to the mixture of the races and cultures that is taken as definitive of Brazilian reality.[17]

Brazilians understand themselves in the eyes of the world not only as mythic sexual beings but also as cannibals. During the modernist period, the leading Brazilian intellectual Oswaldo de Andrade founded the Anthropophagy Movement, writing a "Manifesto antropófago."[18] He proposed that Brazilian artists confirm European suspicions by cannibalizing European aesthetics and culture. The popular culture has its own version of cannibalistic inversions, and they involve the sexual stereotypes as well.

Sex *is* an important, significant element of the carnaval, and not in simple, ecstatic moments of personal abandon. The tourists who flock to Brazil at carnaval time anticipate an orgiastic celebration where individual inhibitions are lifted. But all sexual exchanges during the carnaval—from the theatrical presentation of the bikinied "mulatas" bumping and grinding on the floats in Rio to the actual screwing of a Bahian transvestite and a German tourist behind a stalled trio elétrico— are exchanges within a system of racial, economic, and sexual politics. The stereotyped perception of Brazilian dance—be it samba, deboche, or the bastardized international version of the lambada—as uniformly erotic does not account for the complex historical and cultural meanings of these dances in Brazil. But the juxtaposition of perceived pantomimes of sexual motion with literal acts of sex during the carnaval demands that one acknowledge the erotic aspect of the dances. Still, this eroticism is by no means simple. It directs our attention back toward surrounding political circumstances.

Brazil is a country of shocking economic disparity. The carnaval inversion of rich and poor expresses itself not only in costume but also in sexual exchange. Middle-class whites and poor blacks spend the rest of the year in rigid awareness of their economic roles. Virtually every white household in Bahia has a domestic servant of color. During the carnaval, men and women who would never socialize together are pressed body to body in the deboche, or gyrate hip to hip in the samba. It's true that many middle-class whites refrain from participating in the Bahian street carnaval, preferring the private balls at hotels and country clubs. But many, especially the young, put themselves in the thick of things. In a sweaty, spontaneous, deep, and prolonged kiss, in the massaging of breasts or buttocks which is part of the dance, the deboche, economic disparity seems momentarily healed in a sexual gesture. Of course, it's not. But what this demonstrates is that the dances of the carnaval are not pantomimes of sexuality. Sex, on the contrary, is a gesture choreographed into a dance which signifies vaster social issues.

Economic and racial inversions are not the only ones allowed to occur in the carnaval. There is also a free play of gender roles—particularly for men. On the first night of the Bahian carnaval, for those not scheduled to go out with an official group, the traditional game is transvestism, for both men and women. But men generally take a more enthusiastic part in the switch. Fewer women find fascination in covering themselves up in jackets and ties and painted facial hair. In part, this is because women's transvestism is less readable as such. But it may also be due to the fact that there is significantly less anxiety expressed around the issue of women's flexible sexuality than that of men. On the first night of carnaval, men with lurid eye makeup, inflated breasts, and wobbly high heels fill the square. A man's participation in this event is no indication of his year-round sexual behavior, although it is a moment that suggests that the machista stereotype of

SAMBA

Brazilian straight men covers a more complex sexual identity.[19]

Some of these men, however, are occasional or full-time cross-dressers. The carnaval is understood to be their moment of glory—the brief period in which their sexuality and validity are acknowledged. They are not tolerated, but celebrated. Bahia has a large and famous transvestite population, mostly poor men, black or of mixed race. Many are on hormonal medication, easy to procure in a town where a medical prescription is regarded as an unnecessary scrap of paper in the pharmacies. During the year, Bahian transvestites attract a kind of licentious attention from straight men which is difficult to characterize. They are whistled and hooted at in a manner that seems ironic, aggressive, affectionate, and genuinely sexual all at once. But in the carnaval, men and women alike applaud their beautiful, adolescent-looking breasts, which they expose, for once, with a kind of maternal dignity and pride. In the carnaval, they seem to offer suck of the milk of human tolerance. But their permanently carnivalized position in Brazilian society is hardly a soft one.

The celebration of the transvestite—*travestí* in Portuguese—takes place not only in the street carnaval but in the expensive carnaval balls as well. I have a newspaper account of a 1984 Gay Ball in the exclusive French Meridien Hotel:

> The Gay Ball, at the Meridien on Thursday, was an apotheosis. Inside the hotel, the salon was full, with some costumes actually bought in New York, as was the case of the Royal Peacock, which won in the category of luxury. Outside of the hotel, the evening gang, a fantas-

tic multitude of 300 people, didn't shift a foot until dawn, staying to applaud the transvestites passing by.

There were even tears of emotion, such as those of a public functionary who took her son, a shy *bichinha* [diminutive of bicha], to the ball. When they passed through the aisle formed by the evening gang, they were applauded. "Ai, my son, my eye is full of water. I'm going to cry in there, I never thought it could all be so beautiful. The people applauded me and my son." They were dressed in Sumarian sarongs, both of them.

Of course the melancholy aspect of the story is that the carnaval week is the only week when this bichinha and his mother can expect such a reception.

The term *gay ball* may recall for U.S. readers the events of the same name depicted in Jennie Livingston's film *Paris Is Burning*. The gay balls of Harlem are a black and Latino cultural phenomenon. While enormous interest was provoked by the film's illustration of the complex sexual-identity politics of the competing "houses," surprisingly little has been noted about the specific cultural traditions which frame the balls. The most obvious connection would be with the carnival traditions of black and mixed-race communities throughout the New World. But perhaps a more telling connection could be made to spiritual communities, such as the candomblé communities I have discussed. Gay men, as I have said, have a privileged place in the candomblé. They are capable of embodying principles, in the same way that participants in the Harlem gay balls attempt to "be real"—whether that means a "real" butch queen or a "real" military man.[20] And the father of saints in the candomblé occupies the role generally reserved for the mother, while Harlem house leaders are called, explicitly, mothers of the houses' children.

Judith Butler has mapped what is really at stake in the gay balls, and in transvestism generally:

> drag fully subverts the distinction between inner and outer psychic space and effectively mocks both the expressive model of gender and the notion of a true gender identity. . . . *In imitating gender, drag implicitly reveals the imitative structure of gender itself—as well as its contingency.*[21]

While the embodiment of the orixás in the candomblé is not imitative, it does demonstrate the irrelevance of the specific body in establishing "real" gender. Butler goes on to ask of drag:

> Does this mean that one puts on a mask or a persona, that there is a "one" who precedes that "putting on," who is something other than its gender from the start? Or does this miming, this impersonating precede and form the "one," operating as its formative precondition rather than its dispensable artifice?[22]

The mother of saints would surely respond that there is not "one" but several probably conflicting principles in operation. And the body itself is *both* their formative precondition *and* their dispensable artifice.

Transvestism surrounds the Bahian street carnaval and is the centerpiece of some balls. But the transvestites are not integrated into the organized processional groups—the blocos afro, Indian samba clubs, afoxés, and trios elétricos. The blocos present their kings and queens, skilled African dancers, aboard their floats, and these kings seem to be grand representatives of black masculine ideals. And yet there is an unspoken understanding that while the study of the athletic candomblé choreographies does not indicate femininity in a man, the genuine incorporation of orixá energy in real candomblé dance is typically achieved by women or gay men. But in the carnaval, the choreographies are secularized—and highly stylized. The explicit message of these dances is not one of shifting gender roles. Still, the blocos afro and especially the afoxés, more insistently rooted in the candomblé, hold open a place for the bicha. I used to go to the rehearsals of a small afoxé group in Pelourinho. The group's artistic director was a tough-acting street capoeirista who barked out orders like a sergeant. He was the epitome of the *machão*, ur-macho, violent, inflexible. He stampeded us through our choreographies to the sound of his stamping foot and thunderous claps. But he always acknowledged the expertise of a young, plump bicha with plucked eyebrows who swam through Oxum's seductive moves with supreme grace. Our leader accorded him a special place in our midst. We would watch as he practiced Oxum's solo without music, gliding through her liquid gestures.

The candomblé is a discrete domain which accommodates gays throughout the year. During the carnaval, they—and others—literally come out in a secular moment which is temporally bracketed and therefore unthreatening. The carnaval appears to be a temporally closed circle in the way that the candomblé's circle of faith is both spatially and culturally closed. The terreiro, the physical grounds of the candomblé, is a sanctuary.

SAMBA

My own mother of saints would express mild, ironic disdain for homosexual fathers of saint, and yet as a black woman in Brazil, she, like them, found a sanctuary in her terreiro. She was such a powerful personality, it was hard for me to imagine her shying away from any conflict or difficulty. But I remember her frank face as she told me: "The world outside is crazy. They think I'm crazy for living in here—but I'm not crazy. I lived out there, I know what goes on." I had been living in Rio de Janeiro at the time, and each day as I walked down the sidewalk I'd see the horrifying graphic photos of street violence on the covers of the tabloids. And then, of course, there was the daily spectacle of horrendous economic violences on a people. The insanity of the world "outside" was what drew me to that remarkably peaceful space as well, where jibes were familial, almost comforting, and the fundamental work was one of healing injuries both individual and communal.

"Os Filhos de Gandhy pedem paz"—the Sons of Gandhi ask for peace. This is the banner of my brother organization, and it is a calming phrase which has recurred to me at troublesome moments over the years. Carnaval in Bahia can be a terrifying event. There may be many levels of significance, but the violence is absolutely real. The world outside the carnaval, too, is sometimes brutal beyond belief. So we invoke Mahatma Gandhi, a man of peace. Gandhi is also, of course, a symbol of dignity and resistance in the face of colonial oppression. When his Bahian Sons and Daughters parade in white robes, we are recalling not only

Gandhi but also Oxalá, Big Daddy in the Sky, orixá of the white cloth and of peace.

The Sons and Daughters of Gandhi give another meaning to an African affiliation with Indians—this time, with the great Indian liberator. And the association of Gandhi with Oxalá is a particularly stunning instance of secular syncretism. Gandhi is never embodied in the candomblé. He is a political, historical figure, not an orixá. But he does manifest himself during the carnaval: a frail, bespectacled fellow, dead ringer for the original, says he receives Gandhi's spirit every year, for five days. He rides the float surveying his followers and some-times walks among us. I got pretty friendly with Gandhi myself, as he makes it a habit to get very cozy with his Daughters. Gandhi patted me on the ass! Gently, very gently.

The Sons and Daughters of Gandhi are an alterna-tive version of the Indian nation. We seem to be in stark contrast to the Apaches and the Comanches, but in a way we are all just offering another way of telling a story about Brazil. According to Homi Bhabha,

> Counter-narratives of the nation that continually evoke and erase its totalizing boundaries—both actual and conceptual—disturb those ideological manoeuvres through which "imagined communities" are given essentialist identities.[23]

The Bahian carnaval, I think it is fair to say, blows the lid off of any fixed notion of Brazilianness—as well as Indi-anness and Africanness.

This evocation and erasure of national boundaries is parallel to the evocation and erasure of sexual bound-aries—even the very boundaries of the individual body.

SAMBA

The subversion of national and sexual borders occurs in the candomblé as well, but in the carnaval it is made public, and often violent. In the preceding chapters I have drawn out the complex figures of race in the samba, of sex and sexuality in the candomblé, and of violent struggle in capoeira. But these are not isolated systems of signification. Judith Butler has written of the proliferation of "categories" of political identifications:

> What appear within such an enumerative framework as separable categories are, rather, the conditions of articulation *for* each other: How is race lived in the modality of sexuality? How is gender lived in the modality of race? How do colonial and neo-colonial nation-states rehearse gender relations in the consolidation of state power? How have the humiliations of colonial rule been figured as emasculation (in Fanon), or racist violence as sodomization (JanMohammed); and where and how is "homosexuality" at once the imputed sexuality of the colonized, and the incipient sign of Western imperialism (Walter Williams)? How has the "Orient" been figured as the veiled feminine (Lowe, Chow); and to what extent has feminism pillaged the "Third World" in search of examples of female victimization that would support the thesis of a universal subordination of women (Mohanty)?
>
> And how is it that available discursive possibilities meet their limit in a "subaltern feminine," understood as a catachresis, whose exclusion from representation has become the condition of representation itself (Spivak)? To ask such questions is still to continue to pose the question of "identity," but no longer as a preestablished position or a uniform entity; rather, as part of a dynamic map of power in which identities are constituted and/or erased, deployed and/or paralyzed.[24]

To ask such questions, in fact, is to lay out the dynamic map of the carnaval. Samba *is* a racial history lived in the modality of sexuality. Gender *is* constructed in specifically Afro-Brazilian terms. The nations, African and Indian, commemorated by the blocos and afoxés offer, however, alternative notions of power and gender relations. The humiliations of colonial rule—*and* the humiliation of the homosexual body—are refused. The body of Gandhi, even in its sexualization, is in a sense the veiled feminine, by virtue of its own spiritual penetrability. And it is the capacity of the dancing woman to embody her own spirituality *and* sexuality that counters Western perceptions of patriarchal subordination in the Third World. Finally, it is precisely the woman dancing, the woman I invoked at the beginning of this book, who both seems to preclude and demand our reading of her. I have tried to keep up with her, but her feet move incredibly quickly.

Conclusion

Every closed circle of Brazilian dance is a kind of horizon of safety, a cosmogram of an ideal, isolated world where there is no IMF, no bang-bang, no violent encroachment. And yet of course every roda is also a training ground, and it may be the training ground for fighting. It is not only in the roda de capoeira that one learns to sweep the feet out from under an attacker. The forces on every circle are both centripetal and centrifugal. While the roda de samba seems to expand outward into a secular, even commercial, touristic realm, it continues to reinforce its racial and cultural identity. While the candomblé circle seems to shift under the pressures of Catholicism and other contrary modes of spiritual representation, it holds its ground of community. And while capoeira seems to bust out into jujitsu and break dancing, it is circling back to its origins.

These circles are not merely tangential but also concentric—they contain each other. And as the circle is finally a cosmogram, it is itself, abstractly, uncontainable. In the same way, carnaval, as a specified, contained period of time, expands outward, and finally can't be controlled by a Catholic calendar. The official end, as everyone knows, is Ash Wednesday. But the somber procession of still-drunk, penitent revelers to church to have their foreheads smudged with ash doesn't mean things have really ended.

It is stunning, though, the way in which nature seems to conspire with the church's grim holiday to mark closure. The weeks immediately following carnaval in Bahia are morbidly sad, and it always rains. Children go back to school, the days suddenly seem to shorten drastically, and only the mangled plastic ornaments and the lingering smell of urine hang on for a few days as testament to what happened.

Bahia is tropical, not temperate. But there are seasons: two. Summer is glorious, scorching, brilliant. Winter is just warm, wet, and inexplicably sad. This seasonal change, it seems, is more palpable to the poor. In April, tourists and Bahian playboys and girls continue to frequent the beach. I myself, during the time I lived near the luxury beach, had little sense of a change in the weather, literal or figurative. But when I moved out to the *morro*, the winter filled me with dread. Part of this is eminently explicable: poor neighborhoods are perched on precarious hills (the literal meaning of morro). The houses are shabby constructions that are particularly vulnerable to the mudslides so common in early winter. My own house wasn't very likely to slide anywhere. But there is a winter darkness that is metaphysical—a kind of mudslide of the soul. On the morro after carnaval, gravity pulls one back to certain realities.

I lived in Rio Vermelho, on a morro called o Alto da Sereia—the Mermaid Hill. It was next to Yemanjá's shrine, and stuck out over the bay. The people living there were either poorish by choice (musicians, artists, pot smokers, myself) or just plain poor. My landlord was a soft-faced, sleepy-headed fellow named Gé who lived next door. His big place sometimes turned into a flophouse, when he was feeling ambitious enough to collect payment. He'd run a bar for a while, and before that he'd been a veterinarian, and he liked animal drugs. He wore all white a lot and was a regular Bahian philosopher in the style of Caetano Veloso: New Age hippie with a dose of African righteousness. Gé had some fairly famous musician friends from the days of his bar, and sometimes they would come up the hill to jam. Gé would play half-baked bongos, some of the other intellectuals would join badly in, and the young toughs would look on suspiciously.

One winter evening, the great composer Jorge Mautner came up. Jorge Mautner is an oddball of a Brazilian, from his incongruous name to his bluegrass fiddle playing and his fanatic tai chi training. He's pushing fifty, with a mop of curls, thick spectacles, and a cracked and clefted face. He is the composer of the great socialist anthem "The Color of My Party's Flag Is Red." But the night he came up to my hill, he said, "Let's remember some of those sophisticated old sambas. . . ." There was just a smattering of us hanging out outside of Gé's, slapping mosquitos in the damp, yellow lamplight. Jorge Mautner plucked on a guitar and began to sing one of the oldest Rio samba school songs of all:

> Bangú, city of progress,
> pride of the national style,
> your samba has made its mark.
> Today your name is universal.
> Farewell, Graúju.
> The samba calls me in Bangú.

The samba hung, melancholy, in the moist air. There in the perpetual country of the future, we felt the tinkling of a broken firmament as the present came crashing down to the ground. It was a squalid, muddy little world of contaminated water and jaded kids—and manioc flour was double last month's price, and I had a certain personal problem I couldn't even talk about. Mudslide of the soul!

That is why my favorite celebrations are those that emerge suddenly in the dead of winter, the *festas juninas*, or June feasts. They are one more blast of vitality in a mournful season. These are saints' days—the grandest being Saint John, the second Anthony, patron of impatient aging brides. Like a bachelorette long in the tooth, I learned to look to these saints as hope in a hopeless time. The festas juninas have traditionally celebrated rural northeastern culture—a kind of hillbilly music called *forró*, and foods like boiled peanuts and corn and homemade sugary liqueurs. But in recent years the festas juninas have become another excuse for samba—not grand-scale samba-reggae but small, neighborhood-oriented *samba duro*. Samba duro is an old expression, which can refer to a kind of samba

SAMBA

mixed with capoeira tripups—a sassy, aggressive dance pressing against the limits of fight. But the carnage of recent samba duro is rhythmic, not physical. It is "hard samba" because it keeps shattering its own rhythmic structure. It is very fast, with a more direct, racing clave. Over this rapid-fire pattern, the percussion breaks as fervently and unexpectedly as it can.

The groups that play samba duro are known, simply, as sambas. They may have group T-shirts made, but there is nothing elaborate about their self-presentation. They are the fallout, the radically dispersed, decentralized energy of samba. Neighborhoods love their homegrown sambas, perhaps as intensely as bloco afro members love the great blocos. The festas juninas are their time: the moment of unhierarchical, scattered, amateur samba. Shortly after the night of Jorge Mautner's beautiful, tragic singing on my hill, a nearby morro began its June cycle of samba. The name of that place was *o Morro da Alegria*, the Hill of Happiness, but it was as sad a hill as ours. Still, when the drums began their distant breakage, we were heartened.

The small-time neighborhood groups don't construct a fantasy of riches. They look and act poor. If the samba schools of Rio aim for a regal appearance and "education" (a Brazilian euphemism for money), the sambas of Bahia acknowledge they are simply schools of hard knocks. They lack one kind of elegance, but they also seem to lack the irony of Rio's sambistas. Even the style of the dance is less disciplined: butt out, flat-footed, the dancers joggle through the fast paces seemingly unself-consciously.

But the samba duro can make you swoon with its beauty! A friend of mine brought to New York recently a cassette tape recorded on a Walkman at the rehearsals of the sambas *Leva Eu* (Take Me) and *Samba Fama* (Samba Fame). Despite the distortion and crackling of the tape, a group of us listened, shivering with desire. The rhythmic breaks rolled over each other like waves. Breaking a rhythm is perhaps the most brutal way of calling down orixá energy. But nobody said we were interested in subtlety.

This tape took me back to a June evening in the Valley of Pebbles, several years ago. Boa Gente had organized a competition of sambas on Saint Peter's Day. He'd done this before, but this was the first time groups were coming in from outside the Valley, so he decided to put together a panel of distinguished celebrity judges. I was one. Of course I'm not a celebrity, but Boa could make us what he wanted. With me on the panel were Hugo, a Japanese engineer from São Paulo who was also studying capoeira with Mestre Boa Gente; Sr. Eurico, a Portuguese merchant; Sílvio Mendes, a sportscaster on the local radio; Diogenes, a writer for the local paper; and Mário Silva, singer and composer for the notorious Apaches. The sambas competing were Chega Junto (Arrive Together), Samba Cultura, Os Meninos da Vila (The Boys from the Village), and Beijo com Amor (Kiss with Love).

SAMBA

The other judges and I were led up onto a platform overlooking the crowd, and each of us was supplied with a beer and a score sheet. The truth is, we were already drunk. Boa Gente took the microphone and made an eloquent opening statement in his scratchy, seductive, ironic manner. We were eating from the bowls of salty, hot boiled peanuts which Boa's wife kept sending up. As Boa spoke, you could hear the impatient sambas in the distance warming up.

The clear winner was Beijo. Their samba was raucous, spontaneous, and tasty. They had T-shirts with a picture on the back of two people kissing. Many members carried plastic flowers, which they threw up to me on the platform. Someone seemed to have led them to believe that I was a soap opera star.

After all the groups had performed, we retired to Boa's house for deliberations and more beer. We emerged, trophies were awarded, and Beijo went off to prepare a huge pot of beans. They had vowed to throw a bean party the next day if they won. We had our own pot of *feijoada* waiting for us. Feijoada is the Brazilian national stew, made of black beans and the grisliest parts of a pig or cow you'd care to think of: ears, nose, tail, toes. The parts absorb the rich color of the beans. Boa Gente looked into the pot and said, "Here's the chopped-up body of a black man."

We ate manuscrito (with our hands) from the pot, under the streetlight on the hood of Boa's car. We took a joyride—myself, Boa, Mário, Ivo, Silvana, Bagdad, and the Santos twins. Our appetites whetted from the sambas, we ended up outside Eurico's, making our own rhythm. Someone shouted: "Mothers, keep your daughters locked inside tonight. Mário Silva's playing congas." Mário! With a full belly and a full glass of rum, you put your thick hands to work on that skin. Boa Gente was talking, as usual, hoarse, enchanting, philosophical. He was saying, "We are children, we are dying. . . ." Nights like that, I was always left speechless. I danced. I was listening to the drum without mercy, to the sensible words of the man who understood the terror and the beauty of that samba.

I was listening to the samba talking: "You think this is a game? It is, and yet it's a man's happiness that's at stake. We will commit acts, music, art, sex, violence. Somebody's got to listen. The IMF, the President of the New Republic, you, the reader of this page, have never heard of Mário, or Bagdad, or the Santos twins. We are dying for a little recognition. We are living in the Valley, we are dying, we are children and we are drinking bad water."

Many things I learned in Brazil I learned with my body, and it was only long after that I began to be able to articulate in writing what I had come to understand dancing. Despite our questions as to the political efficacy of carnivalized, ironic inversions or romanticized African fantasies, the insistence of Brazilians to keep *dancing* is not a means of forgetting but rather a perseverance, an unrelenting attempt to intellectualize, theorize, understand a history and a present of social injustice difficult to believe, let alone explain.

Here in New York, it's a lesson I have to keep remembering. Ten years ago, when I was on the prowl in

SAMBA

Central Park with my capoeira pack, it seemed as if our muscular, rhythmic bodies were armor against the world. But in truth, all bodies are open, and vulnerable. In fact, in all likelihood Loremil was already infected with the virus that took him this year. More than anyone, it was he who taught me to dance furiously to keep sorrow at bay. Eminent Bahian, despite his lengthy exile! I learned so much from him that when I found out he was ill and I—painful arbitrariness—was not, I was racked with worry that I had inadvertently sponged off all of his Indian protector spirits. Could they really migrate with such capriciousness?

AIDS, like dance, makes a body significant on a number of levels. In this struggle, the Brazilian community is only beginning to understand what it is up against. And if the people share rhythmic sophistication, elegant choreographies, and the orixás with their African sisters and brothers, they also share deplorable health care, woefully inadequate education, and a lack of available barrier-method birth control. If I could dance Omolú authentically, if he could dance through me, maybe he could make some sense of this. I can't.

The only thing that makes *any* sense to me right now is dancing. It's getting hot. Soon, I'm sure, we'll be making a roda in Central Park—the Bahian rat pack, banging a hip-hop–inflected samba duro out of drums and buckets, with a Portuguese rap in the middle. Bahians in exile are fiercely proud of their culture, even as they mop New York moves and rhythms. This is the *truly* radically dispersed, decentralized energy of samba. It seems like another world, but it's the same one. And if I began by saying my own cultural collision had left me feeling divided, watching them piece together a bicultural polyrhythm has taught me something about healing one's particularity.

Healing, of course, here is a metaphor. I've been talking throughout this book about figures of bodies open (wounded, sexualized, politically or psychically vulnerable) and closed (protected by enclosure in the community). And if I've been arguing that individuals serve themselves well in accepting openness—in rejecting rigid boundaries of identity—then I must acknowledge that the closure of community can be what gives one the strength to do just that.

But as for narrative closure, that's something I'm disinclined to give you. I prefer to end with the samba's perpetual present ("We are children. We are dying"), with Lumidé's tiny, fulsome gesture of Yemanjá collecting the waters, with Gandhi's divine, sublimely gentle pat.

Notes

Introduction

1. Claude Lévi-Strauss, *Tristes tropiques*, trans. John Russell (New York: Criterion, 1961), p. 58.

2. The melancholia and loss of the voyage to Brazil in *Tristes tropiques* is colored by Lévi-Strauss's subsequent exile from France, which was occasioned not by any choice of displacement but by the Nazi occupation.

3. See Jane Gallop, *Thinking through the Body* (New York: Columbia University Press, 1988).

4. See Houston Baker, Jr., *Workings of the Spirit* (Chicago: University of Chicago Press, 1991).

5. Note, in particular, the work of Rosângela Sylvestre, a choreographer and dance scholar working in New York. Sylvestre choreographs in a style she has termed Contemporary Afro-Brazilian, which reflects the interaction of Western and traditional forms.

6. Paul Rabinow, "Representations Are Social Facts," in James Clifford and George Marcus, eds., *Writing Culture: The*

Poetics and Politics of Ethnography (Berkeley: University of California Press, 1986), p. 258.

7. Margaret Thompson Drewal, *Yoruba Ritual: Performers, Play, Agency* (Bloomington: Indiana University Press, 1992).

8. Paulin Hountondji, *African Philosophy: Myth and Reality* (Bloomington: Indiana University Press, 1983). On the "African scholar's burden," see also Abiola Irele, "The African Scholar," *Transition* 51 (1991), pp. 56–69.

9. Henry Louis Gates, Jr., *The Signifying Monkey* (New York: Oxford University Press, 1988).

10. Maya Deren, *Divine Horsemen: The Living Gods of Haiti* (New York: Dell, 1970; reprint, New Paltz, N.Y.: Documentext, McPherson, 1983), pp. 323–24.

11. Karen McCarthy Brown, *Mama Lola* (Berkeley: University of California Press, 1991), p. 11.

12. The 1980s Hollywood film *The Believers* has encoded even this seemingly innocent term into a history of hateful, fear-mongering cinematic depictions of pan-African religion. I place quotation marks around the word *believer* to forestall such a reading.

13. James Clifford, *The Predicament of Culture* (Cambridge: Harvard University Press, 1988), p. 24.

14. Clifford and Marcus, eds., *Writing Culture*.

15. Lila Abu-Lughod, "Can There Be a Feminist Ethnography?" *Women and Performance* 5 (1990), no. 1, p. 18.

1. Samba

1. Edison Carneiro, the anthropologist, writes: "the choreography of the samba is characterized by a slippery step, by individual creativity, and by no other fixed rule than that all that the sambista feels must be *said*, must be expressed, with the feet." *Carta do Samba* (Rio de Janeiro: Ministerio da Educação e Cultura, 1962), p. 11 (my translation). The expression is a commonplace.

2. For a discussion of basic narratological principles, see Tzvetan Todorov, "The Two Principles of Narrative," trans. Philip E. Lewis, *Diacritics* 1 (Fall 1971).

3. See Robert Toplin, *The Abolition of Slavery in Brazil* (New York: Atheneum, 1972), and Robert Conrad, *The Destruction of Brazilian Slavery, 1850–1888* (Berkeley: University of California Press, 1972).

4. Thomas E. Skidmore, *Black into White: Race and Nationality in Brazilian Thought* (New York: Oxford University Press, 1974).

5. Francisco José de Oliveira Vianna, *Evolução do povo brasileiro* (São Paulo: Companhia Editoria Nacional, 1938).

6. Gilberto Freyre, *New World in the Tropics: The Culture of Modern Brazil* (New York: Knopf, 1959), p. 119.

7. Ibid., p. 146.

8. Skidmore, *Black into White*, p. 192.

9. Dante Moreira Leite, *O Caráter nacional brasileiro* (São Paulo: Pioneira, 1969), p. 271. See also Carlos Guilherme Mota, *Ideologia da cultura brasileira: 1933–1974* (São Paulo: Editora Atica, 1978).

10. Freyre, *New World*, p. 119.

11. Oracy Nogueira, *Tanto preto quanto branco: Estudos de relações raciáis* (São Paulo: T.A. Queiroz, 1985).

12. Carlos Hasenbalg, "Race Relations in Post-Abolition Brazil: The Smooth Preservation of Racial Inequalities," Ph.D. dissertation, University of California, Berkeley, 1978, p. 258.

13. Thomas E. Skidmore, "Race Relations in Brazil," *Camões Center Quarterly* 4, nos. 3 and 4 (1992–93), p. 49.

14. Abdías do Nascimento, *O Negro revoltado* (Rio de Janeiro: Editora GRD, 1968).

15. Florestan Fernandes, *The Negro in Brazilian Society*, trans. Jacqueline D. Skiles, A. Brunel, and Arthur Rothwell (New York: Columbia University Press, 1969).

16. For a consideration of some of the challenges of modern dance ethnography, see Anya Peterson Royce, *The Anthropology of Dance* (Bloomington: Indiana University Press, 1989), pp. 17–37.

SAMBA

17. The semiotic aspect of my analysis is greatly indebted to Muniz Sodré's small and beautiful book, *Samba, o dono do corpo* (Rio de Janeiro: Codecri, 1979). Sodré's thesis, with which I am clearly in accord, is that samba is inherently semiological and constitutes a language in response to cultural repression. He notes that the clue to this language is encoded in the name of the very first samba school of the Rio carnaval: Deixa Falar—"let me speak." I hope here merely to expand this discussion in order to accommodate for the development of the language over time.

18. Robert F. Thompson, "An Aesthetic of the Cool: West African Dance," *African Forum* 2, no. 2 (Fall 1966), pp. 93–94.

19. John Miller Chernoff, *African Rhythm and African Sensibility* (Chicago: University of Chicago Press, 1979), p. 50.

20. Olavo Bilac, *Kosmos* (1906), cited in Baptista Siqueira, *Origem do termo samba* (São Paulo: IBRASA, 1977), p. 138 (my translation).

21. See Benjamin Nuñez, *Dictionary of Afro-Latin Civilization* (Westport, Conn.: Greenwood Press, 1980).

22. Edison Carneiro, *Folguedos tradicionáis* (Rio de Janeiro: Conquista, 1974), pp. 35–36.

23. Carl Degler, *Neither Black nor White: Slavery and Race Relations in Brazil* (Madison: University of Wisconsin Press, 1971), p. xii.

24. Ibid., p. 225. On the multiracialism of Brazil, see also Marvin Harris, *Patterns of Race in the Americas* (New York: Walter, 1964).

25. Gilberto Freyre, *The Masters and the Slaves: A Study in the Development of Brazilian Civilization*, trans. Samuel Putnam (Berkeley: University of California Press, 1986), p. 323.

26. See J. Michael Turner, "Brown into Black: Changing Racial Attitudes of Afro-Brazilian Students," in Pierre Michel Fontaine, ed., *Race, Class and Power in Brazil* (Los Angeles: Center for Afro-American Studies, UCLA, 1985), pp. 73–94.

27. The up-and-coming mixed-race pop star Carlinhos Brown dubbed himself a Brazilian Charlie Brown not after the comic strip character but after his own skin and James Brown,

a major figure (along with traditional Afro-Bahian percussion) in his musical formation.

28. Raúl Lody, *Samba de caboclo* (Rio de Janeiro: Funarte, 1977), p. 5 (my translation).

29. "I am colored but I offer nothing in the way of extenuating circumstances except the fact that I am the only Negro in the United States whose grandfather on the mother's side was *not* an Indian chief." Zora Neale Hurston, "How It Feels to Be Colored Me," in *I Love Myself When I Am Laughing and Then Again When I Am Looking Mean and Impressive*, ed. Alice Walker (Old Westbury, N.Y.: Feminist Press, 1979), p. 152.

30. Michael Taussig, *Shamanism, Colonialism, and the Wild Man: A Study in Terror and Healing* (Chicago: University of Chicago Press, 1986).

31. See Jim Wafer, *The Taste of Blood: Spirit Possession in the Brazilian Candomblé* (Philadelphia: University of Pennsylvania Press, 1991), esp. pp. 53–87.

32. Maria Teixeira, *O Rodar das rodas: Dos homens e dos orixás* (Rio de Janeiro: Instituto Nacional do Folclore, 1985), pp. 46–47.

33. Ibid., p. 33.

34. Sodré, *Samba*.

35. Frantz Fanon, *The Wretched of the Earth*, trans. Constance Farrington (New York: Grove Press, 1968), p. 84.

2. Divine Choreography and the Embodiment of Metaphor

1. Royce, *Anthropology of Dance*, describes Laban's influence in the field of dance ethnography.

2. Ishmael Reed, *Mumbo Jumbo* (New York: Atheneum, 1972), p. 211.

3. See Wande Abimbola, *Ifá: An Exposition of Ifá Literary Corpus* (Ibadan: Oxford University Press, 1977), and Júlio Braga, *O Jogo de búzios: Um estudo de adivinhação no candomblé* (São Paulo: Brasiliense, 1988).

4. See Robert F. Thompson, *Flash of the Spirit* (New York: Vintage, 1984), pp. 113–16.

5. Surely the site of cicatrization most painful for the ethnologist to acknowledge is that of female circumcision, a practice not as common or as extreme among the Yoruba as among, for example, the Sudanese. But any instance of female circumcision (a practice overseen by worshipers of Ogun) must force the Westerner to hold her desires for "cultural relativism" side by side with her notions of fundamental women's rights. Gayatri Chakravorty Spivak raises this issue in *In Other Worlds* (New York: Routledge, 1988), pp. 134–53.

6. See Henry John Drewal, "Art or Accident: Yoruba Body Artists and Their Deity Ogun," in Sandra T. Barnes, ed. *Africa's Ogun* (Bloomington: Indiana University Press, 1989), pp. 235–60.

7. The initiate in candomblé is said to have a *corpo fechado*, or "closed body," which would reinforce the idea of a doubled healing. Prior to the cut, the individual is vulnerable, but the very wounding which occurs in the initiation offers protection. The alternation and exchange of figures for bodily hermeticism and openness will become increasingly important later in this chapter.

8. This is the account of syncretism held by most worshipers in the candomblé. However, it is not universally accepted. As black political consciousness is rising, so is resistance to the narrative of African accommodation. One of the most outspoken detractors of syncretism is the mother of saints Stella Azevedo, of the famous house Ilê Axé Opô Afonjá. In 1986 she delivered a paper at an international conference in New York on Oriṣa culture, arguing that syncretism was necessitated by the cultural violences of slavery, and today candomblé should strive for African purity. This condemnation of the "impure" is articulated to varying degrees is several of the more conservative houses, as well as in the earlier ethnographic literature.

9. Deren, *Divine Horsemen*, p. 230.

10. See Margaret Thompson Drewal, "Dancing for Ogun in Yorubaland and in Brazil," in Barnes, ed., *Africa's Ogun*, pp. 199–234.

11. Deren, *Divine Horsemen*, p. 228.

12. Drewal, "Dancing for Ogun," p. 225.

13. See Freyre, *The Masters and the Slaves*.

14. Ruth Landes, *City of Women* (New York: Macmillan, 1947), p. 37.

15. Ruth Landes, "A Cult Matriarchate and Male Homosexuality," *Journal of Abnormal and Social Psychology* 35, no. 3 (1940), pp. 386–97, my emphasis.

16. Roger Bastide, *O Candomblé da Bahia* (São Paulo: Editora Nacional, 1961), p. 309.

17. See Peter Fry, "Da hierarquia a igualdade: A construção da homossexualidade no Brasil," in Fry, ed., *Para Inglês ver: Identidade e política na cultura brasileira* (Rio de Janeiro: Zahar Editores, 1982), pp. 87–115, and Richard Parker, *Bodies, Pleasures, and Passions: Sexual Culture in Contemporary Brazil* (Boston: Beacon Press, 1991). On homosexuality in the candomblé, see Fry, "Homossexualidade masculina e cultos afro-brasileiros," in Fry, ed., *Para Inglês ver*, pp. 54–86.

18. Lorand Matory, "Homens montados: Homossexualidade e simbolismo da possessão nas religioes afro-brasileiras," in J.J. Reis, ed., *Escravidão e invenção da liberdade: Estudos sobre o Negro no Brasil* (São Paulo: Brasiliense, 1988), pp. 215–31.

19. Judith Butler, *Gender Trouble: Feminism and the Subversion of Identity* (New York: Routledge, 1990), p. 132.

20. Wafer, *Taste of Blood*, p. 106.

21. Ibid.

22. Hélène Cixous and Cathérine Clément, *The Newly Born Woman*, trans. Betsy Wing (Minneapolis: University of Minnesota Press, 1986), p. 86.

23. Ibid., pp. 85–86.

24. Just how much is at stake in incorporating divinity is perhaps illustrated by one of the weirdest and, to me, most poignant moments in Deren's *Divine Horsemen*. In describing

SAMBA

the qualities of the loa Ghede, consumer and bestower of vitality, unpredictable arbiter of the grave and lascivious macho glutton, Deren recounts his intervention in the illness of a little girl. After all treatments both European and traditional had failed, the girl's priestess undertook a ceremony for Ghede. "Strong" blood offerings were made, and the ceremony was attended by a number of other priestesses as well as family and other initiates.

> With this evidence of devotion, Ghede agreed to intervene. He possessed one of the mambos, and asked that the child be brought out and placed on the tomb. He took the blood of the goat and, undressing the child, anointed her with it. Then, singing fervently, he reached down between his legs and brought forth, in his cupped palm, a handful of fluid with which he washed the child. It was not urine. And though it would seem impossible that this should be so, since it was a female body which he had possessed, it was a seminal ejaculation. Again and again he gave of that life fluid, and bathed the child with it, while the mambos and hounsis sang and wept with gratitude for this ultimate gesture. Of the life which he had in the past consumed, he now gave forth in full measure. And though there is no reasonable way to account for this, the child lived. (Pp. 113–114)

I myself have never witnessed such a transformation of the secreting powers of the divine body in Brazil. Perhaps this is because the loa, unlike the orixás, are not hermetic: they eat, sometimes voraciously, and consequently are able to secrete as well. I certainly have seen plenty of "unexplainable" events, and I have seen women and men in the candomblé so surely embodying characteristics different from "their own" that my understanding of identity has been irreversibly altered.

25. See Gates's extended meditation on this figure in *The Signifying Monkey*.

26. Drewal, "Dancing for Ogun," p. 227.

27. Thompson, *Flash of the Spirit*, p. 65.

28. It was subsequent to writing this description that I read Wafer's:

> When Oxum, who is the mirror, combs her flowing hair
> in front of her mirror, what does she see? Is it a woman,
> or is it a man? Is her skin white, or is it black? Does she
> see youth, beauty, love, wealth, and life; or age,
> ugliness, hatred, poverty, and death? Do her head and
> her tail see these things as different? Or does this
> creature of conjunctions have a simultaneous vision of
> what, for us mortals, are perspectival inversions or
> temporal transformations? (*Taste of Blood*, p. 22)

The fact that Oxum seems to tempt one to describe her in suspended (irresolvable) rhetorical questions would appear to be related to the principle of self-reflexivity.

29. Judith Gleason invokes this sensation in a work dedicated to Iansã and her metaphysical motion: "Caught in her updrafts, the religious imagination without apparatus seeks rather to meet the weather goddess halfway, where sensuous experience is still possible. By reconnecting ourselves to the elements through which her urgent temperament expresses itself in patterns recognizable in our own swirls, inundations, and disjunctive ardors, we come upon a common language with which to invoke and reflect her power." *Oyá: In Praise of the Goddess* (Boston: Shambhala, 1987), pp. 17–18.

30. "Having visited the winds, having seized our part of fire, having felt those convective currents coursing through our veins, we are ready to take on the thing itself—unaccommodated storm. In theory, it shouldn't be all that difficult for a woman to own the storm, essentially an invaginative process." Ibid., p. 35.

31. See Thompson, *Flash of the Spirit*, pp. 42–43.

32. Wafer, *Taste of Blood*, pp. 85–86.

33. See ibid., p. 87.

SAMBA

3. Headspin

1. The English verb *to play* can be translated three ways in Portuguese: *brincar* (intransitive) = to play freely, like a child; *jogar* (transitive) = to play a sport or game; or *tocar* (transitive) = to play a musical instrument. Capoeira may appear to be a physical game or sport, but, as John Lowell Lewis has pointed out, all three kinds of play are demanded of the capoeirista, who must be an athlete, a musician in his own accompaniment, and—at the highest levels—a master of childish imagination. See Lewis, *Ring of Liberation: Deceptive Discourse in Brazilian Capoeira* (Chicago: University of Chicago Press, 1992), p. 2.

2. See, for example, Bira Almeida, *Capoeira, a Brazilian Art Form* (Palo Alto: Sun Wave, 1981).

3. I discuss later in this chapter the distinction between *angola* and *regional* styles, as well as the counterarguments to their division.

4. See Robert F. Thompson, "Capoeira," New York, Capoeira Foundation, 1988; Kenneth Dossar, "Capoeira Angola: Dancing between Two Worlds," *Afro-Hispanic Review* 11, nos. 1–3 (1992), pp. 5–10; and Gerhard Kubik, "Angolan Traits in Black Music, Games and Dances of Brazil: A Study of African Cultural Extensions Overseas," *Estudos de Antropologia Cultural*, no. 10 (Lisbon, 1979), pp. 7–55.

5. Thomas H. Holloway, "'A Healthy Terror': Police Repression of *Capoeiras* in Nineteenth-Century Rio de Janeiro," *Hispanic American Historical Review* 69 (1989), p. 643. Waldeloir Rego, *Capoeira Angola, ensaio socio-etnográfico* (Salvador: Editora Itapuã, 1968), pp. 17–29, gives a fairly extensive account of the debate, which is summarized and modified in Lewis, *Ring of Liberation*, pp. 42–44. See also Bira Almeida, *Capoeira*, pp. 17–20.

6. Kubik, "Angolan Traits," p. 29.

7. See Décio Freitas, *Palmares, a guerra dos escravos* (Rio de Janeiro: 1982).

8. Lewis, *Ring of Liberation*, p. 38, expresses skepticism about this historical narrative while acknowledging its cultural significance.

9. See Bira Almeida, *Capoeira*, and Rego, *Capoeira Angola*.

10. Quoted in Raimundo Cesar Alves de Almeida, *Bimba: Perfil do mestre* (Salvador: UFBA, 1982), pp. 13–14.

11. Alma Guillermoprieto recounts a disturbing history of political and financial manipulation and corruption at the leadership level of the samba schools in Rio. See her *Samba* (New York: Knopf, 1990).

12. John Guillory's considerations of multiculturalism and canon formation are most instructive on this point. He warns that limiting the discussion to what is included in or excluded from the canon can obfuscate the greater question of pedagogy: "To have drawn up a new syllabus is not yet to have begun teaching, nor is it yet to have begun reflection upon the institutional form of the school." Guillory, "Canon, Syllabus, List: A Note on the Pedagogic Imaginary," *Transition* 52 (1992), p. 54.

13. Edison Carneiro, *Capoeira* (Rio de Janeiro: Ministério da Educação e Cultura, 1975), p. 14.

14. See Lewis, *Ring of Liberation*, p. 62.

15. Ibid., p. 64.

16. Bira Almeida, *Capoeira*, p. 115 n.

17. Raimundo Almeida, *Bimba*, p. 18.

18. Bira Almeida, *Capoeira*, p. 1.

19. Mestre Vicente Ferreira Pastinha, LP recording, *Capoeira Angola*.

20. Thompson, *Flash of the Spirit*, pp. 113–16.

21. Ibid., p. 108.

22. Kenneth Dossar explicitly links the aú to Kongo games that act out a "dance between two worlds," that of the

living and the dead, by inverting the body. See Dossar, "Capoeira Angola."

23. Pastinha, LP recording.

24. For a sample of the wide variety, see Bira Almeida, *Capoeira*.

25. Lewis, *Ring of Liberation*, p. 159.

26. Pastinha, LP recording.

27. Lewis, *Ring of Liberation*, p. 73, discusses the gender barrier, although he perhaps exaggerates it (not acknowledging, for example, Edna Lima's work).

28. Dossar, "Capoeira Angola," p. 5.

29. See my discussion of the orixá Ogun in the preceding chapter.

30. Jorge Amado, *Bahia de Todos os Santos* (Rio de Janeiro: Record, 1980).

31. See chap. 1 on this term.

32. Lewis writes that the taxonomy of "attacks" and "defense moves" is never clear. Many moves "can function *either* as attacks or defenses, or even as *both* at the same time!" Lewis, *Ring of Liberation*, p. 98.

33. Jaír Moura, "Capoeiragem—Arte e malandragem," *Cadernos de Cultura*, no. 2 (Salvador, 1980), pp. 15–16.

34. Amos Tutuola, *The Palm-Wine Drinkard* (New York: Grove Press, 1984), p. 35.

35. Kenneth Dossar, "Capoeira Angola: An Ancestral Connection?" *American Visions* 3, no. 4 (1988), pp. 38–42.

36. See my argument on the "pressure-valve" theory of carnaval in the next chapter.

4. Of the Daughters of Gandhi

1. Parker, *Bodies, Pleasures, and Passions*, p. 7.

2. See chap. 1.

3. See Barbara Browning, "Retracing the *Figure Humaine:* The Inverted Designs of French Ethnographic Human-

ism on the Face of the Brazilian Savage," Ph.D. dissertation, Yale University, 1989.

4. Pêro Vaz de Caminha, in Leonardo Arroyo, ed., *A Carta de Pêro de Caminha: Ensaio de informação à procura de constantes válidas de método* (Rio de Janeiro: Edições Melhoramentos, 1971), p. 78.

5. Daniel Crowley, *African Myth and Black Reality in Bahian Carnival* (Los Angeles: Museum of Cultural History, UCLA, Monograph Series 25, 1984), p. 26.

6. Christopher Dunn, "Afro-Bahian Carnival: A Stage for Protest," *Afro-Hispanic Review* 11, nos. 1–3 (1992), p. 12.

7. Steven Feierman, "African Histories and the Dissolution of World History," in Robert H. Bates, V. Y. Mudimbe, and Jean O'Barr, eds., *Africa and the Disciplines: The Contributions of Research in Africa to the Social Sciences and Humanities* (Chicago: University of Chicago Press, 1993), p. 169.

8. This episode was memorialized in the classic account of Euclides da Cunha, *Rebellion in the Backlands*, trans. Samuel Putnam (Chicago: University of Chicago Press, 1944).

9. See Dunn, "Afro-Bahian Carnival," p. 19 n. 1.

10. See, in particular, Roberto Da Matta, *Carnivals, Rogues, & Heroes: An Interpretation of the Brazilian Dilemma*, trans. John Drury (Notre Dame: University of Notre Dame Press, 1991).

11. See Guillermoprieto, *Samba*.

12. See Sam Kinser, *Carnival, American Style: Mardi Gras at New Orleans and Mobile* (Chicago: University of Chicago Press, 1990), and Jason Berry, Jonathan Foose, and Tad Jones, *Up from the Cradle of Jazz* (Athens: University of Georgia Press, 1986).

13. George Lipsitz, "Mardi Gras Indians: Carnival and Counter-Narrative in Black New Orleans," *Cultural Critique* 10 (Fall 1988), pp. 99–121.

14. Dunn, "Afro-Bahian Carnival," p. 14.

15. Daniel Touro Linger, *Dangerous Encounters: Meanings of Violence in a Brazilian City* (Stanford: Stanford University Press, 1992), p. 13.

16. Parker, *Bodies, Pleasures, and Passions*, p. 163.

17. Ibid., p. 149.

18. Oswaldo de Andrade, "Manifesto antropófago," in *Trechos escolhidos* (Rio de Janeiro: AGIR, 1967).

19. Again, the most detailed discussion is in Parker, *Bodies, Pleasures, and Passions*. See also João Trevisan, *Perverts in Paradise* (London: GMP, 1986).

20. I had the opportunity in 1992 to ask one of the stars of *Paris Is Burning*, Willi Ninja, about his view of the relationship between the balls and Afro–New World traditions of spirit possession. I was surprised but intrigued by his response. Rather than addressing specific cultural influences, he described his own trancelike experiences in the balls, where he was both supremely aware of his bodily motion (Ninja is perhaps the outstanding voguer of all times, capable of incredibly precise and agile moves), and yet "outside" his body at the same time.

21. Judith Butler, *Bodies That Matter: On the Discursive Limits of "Sex"* (New York: Routledge, 1993), p. 137.

22. Ibid., p. 230.

23. Homi K. Bhabha, ed., *Nation and Narration* (New York: Routledge, 1990), p. 300.

24. Butler, *Bodies That Matter*, p. 117.

Index

SAMBA

SAMBA

SAMBA

Barbara Browning teaches in the Department of Performance Studies at New York University. She has studied, taught, and performed Brazilian dance in Brazil, the United States, and Europe.